As we celebrate the start of the year 2020 environmental hazards and strain in int level lurks the sad news of the loss of a loved one and the abducting of a 20-year-old daughter of a close family friend by Boko Haram in Maiduguri, Nigeria. The harsh realities of a broken world can either drive us to despair or pretence. In despairing we seem hopeless; in pretending we lie. Even the neatest of theological paradigms can let us down with regard to answers in the face of real suffering.

In *Stumbling Toward Zion: Recovering the Biblical Tradition of Lament in the Era of World Christianity*, Dr David Smith brings an age-old biblical tradition back on the table. He points out biblical examples of what was sometimes a long and hard struggle between things promised or hoped for and fears arising from a contradicting reality. Such tension between promise and brokenness is still with us to this day.

In affirming the spirituality of lament, Dr Smith helps us to see how the troubles of a broken world can interact with the reliable promises of a faithful God. He bravely ventures into thoughtful expressions on how the understanding of biblical modes of lament can be insightful basis for real hope and change. The book rightfully reckons with Christianity today as being increasingly shaped by the experiences of non-Western communities. While acknowledging that human suffering is universal, this book brims with examples of adversity from non-Western contexts, underscoring how such hardship can breed unique perspectives on the spirituality of lament, thereby leading to hopes of social transformation and healing.

For all who yearn to see a bridge in the gap between faith and suffering, promise and reality, vision and limitation, divinity and humanity, through deep reflections on prayerful lament, this book is a very promising read. Dr Smith's reflection is also a brotherly solidarity with many around the world who find it hard to "sing the Lord's song in a strange land."

Samuel O. N. G. Nwokoro
Lecturer in Early Christian-Muslim Relations and Church History,
Department of Public Theology,
Theological College of Northern Nigeria, Jos, Nigeria

Stumbling toward Zion is an outstanding book that makes a unique contribution to *Recovering the Biblical Tradition of Lament in the Era of World Christianity*. There is a deep authenticity about David Smith's approach. He listens carefully to the biblical text, is attentive to a rich diversity of voices from the Majority World church and crucially, demonstrates an honest and vulnerable spirituality in his own writing. After reading this stunning work, the reader is left in no doubt that the church in the West must recover the biblical tradition of praise and lament if its witness is to be in any way authentic for our twenty-first-century contexts. A critical factor in that recovery, as Smith points out, is the Western church's willingness to listen to the global chorus singing new songs from the world Christian movement across the southern hemisphere. It is in those contexts that we see a spirituality of lament connecting with a broken world in such ways that the church in its worship and witness embodies the good news of Christ crucified, buried and raised. I warmly commend this book and its author.

Peter Rowan, PhD
Co-National Director, OMF (UK)

Stumbling toward Zion offers a penetrating analysis regarding the loss of lament amidst global and cultural changes that are overtaking Christian faith and witness. The book is pregnant with biblical scholarship and insights from the world church; David Smith weaves personal stories of loss and hope and includes thoughts for reflection at the end of each chapter. I recommend this treasured gift warmly to mission workers and church leaders for careful study and application.

Kang-San Tan, PhD
General Director, BMS World Mission

Stumbling toward Zion

Langham
GLOBAL LIBRARY

Stumbling toward Zion

Recovering the Biblical Tradition of Lament
in the Era of World Christianity

David W. Smith

GLOBAL LIBRARY

© 2020 David W. Smith

Published 2020 by Langham Global Library
An imprint of Langham Publishing
www.langhampublishing.org

Langham Publishing and its imprints are a ministry of Langham Partnership

Langham Partnership
PO Box 296, Carlisle, Cumbria, CA3 9WZ, UK
www.langham.org

ISBNs:
978-1-78368-777-0 Print
978-1-78368-819-7 ePub
978-1-78368-820-3 Mobi
978-1-78368-821-0 PDF

David W. Smith has asserted his right under the Copyright, Designs and Patents Act, 1988 to be identified as the Author of this work.

All rights reserved. No part of this publication may be reproduced, stored in a retrieval system or transmitted, in any form or by any means, electronic, mechanical, photocopying, recording or otherwise, without the prior written permission of the publisher or the Copyright Licensing Agency.

Requests to reuse content from Langham Publishing are processed through PLSclear. Please visit www.plsclear.com to complete your request.

Scripture quotations are taken from the Holy Bible, New International Version®, Anglicised, NIV®. Copyright © 1979, 1984, 2011 by Biblica, Inc®. Used by permission. All rights reserved worldwide.

British Library Cataloguing-in-Publication Data
A catalogue record for this book is available from the British Library

ISBN: 978-1-78368-777-0

Cover & Book Design: projectluz.com

Cover Image: Painting by Anneke Kaai – *Psalm 119 : 105* from series *In a Word*. www.annekekaai.nl

Langham Partnership actively supports theological dialogue and an author's right to publish but does not necessarily endorse the views and opinions set forth here or in works referenced within this publication, nor can we guarantee technical and grammatical correctness. Langham Partnership does not accept any responsibility or liability to persons or property as a consequence of the reading, use or interpretation of its published content.

For all who suffer the absence of God and experience the pain of his silence, longing for the renewed presence of the Father who comforts those who mourn and runs to embrace his returning children.

CONTENTS

Foreword

I have long been an admirer of David Smith's writings, since he brings together wide literary and theological reading with deep reflections drawn from his long cross-cultural missionary experience. Moreover, since my wife died in May 2018, David and I have been in regular email correspondence and on Skype, sharing our experiences of bereavement and the deep dismay we have both felt over the superficiality of much evangelical worship and preaching, particularly in churches removed from the daily agony of peoples ravaged by chronic illness, poverty, unemployment, violence and war.

David's present book addresses head-on that superficiality, indeed, evasion of the pain, anger and doubt that we find running through the biblical writings and, if we are honest, central to every Christian's experience. David takes us on a survey of relevant Old and New Testament material, and constantly relates his exposition to the global political and economic powers against which we struggle today. To illustrate his themes he not only marshals biblical and theological arguments but draws on his musical and artistic knowledge. I was so moved by his description of the sixteenth-century Isenheim altarpiece by Mathis Grunewald that, on a trip to France, I made a special detour to the French-German border town of Colmar to see it for myself. David's commentary enriched the sense of awe I felt gazing at the crucified figure.

This, then, is a book that will provoke, enlighten, comfort and inspire a hope that is the opposite of a shallow optimism. It should be read by all who hunger for honest theology.

Vinoth Ramachandra, PhD
IFES International Secretary for Dialogue & Social Engagement
Colombo, Sri Lanka

Preface

The titles authors give to their books often suggest something concerning their journeys through life. Nearly twenty years ago I published a small book with the title *Crying in the Wilderness: Evangelism and Mission in Today's Culture*. The explicit nature of that title made clear my central concerns at the time: I was wrestling with the future of the Christian mission in the context of a rapidly changing world and asking questions concerning the need for change if the challenges presented to the gospel by contemporary culture were to be met. Now, almost two decades later, this present book bears a title which testifies to the continuing struggle with the same kinds of issues, but this time it is rather more ambiguous, so the reader deserves some explanation at this point.

For almost fifty years I had the privilege of sharing life and service with my wife, Joyce. The reader will discover within the following pages occasional references to our experiences which I have used in this book to illustrate the importance to us of the biblical tradition of the prayer of lament. Our realization of the crucial importance of lament deepened over many years and through a variety of contexts in which we were personally exposed to suffering or, more often, became aware of the extent of the extremity of pain and loss suffered by other people. For me the climax of this path of discovery came with Joyce's own terminal illness and death from a brain tumour which brought an extended period of shared distress. Toward the end of her life I was called to her bedside by nursing staff on a couple of occasions and was asked to remain with her through the night. During one of these vigils as I sat beside her I found myself singing the words of a long-forgotten song: "We're marching to Zion." She opened her eyes and joined in with me: "We're marching upward to Zion, the beautiful city of God."

It was, as may be imagined, a precious moment and one for which I will remain forever grateful. However, after her passing I found myself reflecting on those words and wondering about the term "marching." Quite apart from the fact that I have always had an aversion to the use of militaristic language in relation to Christianity and its mission, that terminology simply did not reflect the reality of my experience. In fact, even during Joyce's illness I had struggled with God and what seemed to be his silence. On another of those night vigils I had listened to her crying out to Jesus in the darkness, begging him to restore strength to her legs, and I found myself asking why, if the lame were made to walk in Galilee, did those anguished prayers seem to go unanswered? This was one of many "stumbles" on my own journey toward Zion.

If the original inspiration for my title came from personal experience, I have come to realize that the theme of lament is of far wider significance and has crucial importance in relation to the life and testimony of the Christian movement throughout the world in the twenty-first century. All my work has been concerned with the struggle to discern the nature of the still-emerging paradigm of Christian identity and testimony in a time of massive change and uncertainty, and it has become ever more obvious to me that the transformation demanded of Christianity today involves far more than structural and organizational changes. It relates above all to fundamental issues concerning Christian identity and the outworking of the core values which flow from our confession of Jesus Christ as Lord. This is, as I try to show in the following pages, an era of unprecedented danger and uncertainty, which at the same time presents an extraordinary opportunity for the emergence of a different kind of global movement, one that might be capable of offering our broken world an alternative model of life together within the human family. If we are to meet this challenge we will need all the resources provided for us by the gospel, including the biblical tradition of praise and lament which has the potential to transform our worship, deepen our spirituality and renew our communities so that they become spheres of honesty, hope and healing.

Readers should be warned that the following pages contain some radical criticisms of contemporary expressions of the Christian faith, and especially of what seems to me to be the triumphalism and complacency of so much public worship in the churches of Europe and North America. The one-sided emphasis on celebration not only ignores the suffering, struggles and doubts of people within congregations, so increasing their distress by making them feel guilty that they are unable to join the party, but, even more seriously, it suppresses knowledge of the crises threatening the very survival of our world and so undermines the credibility of faith in the eyes of suffering people who are searching for genuine hope. I will argue in the following pages that there is need for radical transformation in contemporary Christianity, especially in the Western world, amounting to a reconversion which could result in new depths of spirituality, a fresh understanding of the nature of the gospel and a new kind of counter-cultural praxis in a world controlled by false gods and moving toward apocalypse.

Finally, the reference to "world Christianity" in my title indicates the central importance of this phenomenon within the following discussion. If the malaise which I discern within the Christianity of Europe and North America forms one major strand within this book, the other relates to the huge significance of the character and promise of the Christian faith in its new heartlands across the Majority World. It is what happens there which will determine the future of Christianity as a world religion, and a major motivation of this book is the desire to alert believers in the secular West to the extent and significance of what has been called the "new Reformation." This is overwhelmingly a movement "from below," from the margins of the globalized world, among poor and disenfranchised peoples, many living in slum conditions in ever-expanding megacities or in depopulated villages from which the young have fled. As the following pages will show, in such places the lament remains very much alive, both because it expresses the anguish and trauma which is so often part of everyday experience in Africa, Latin America and Asia, and because it gives birth to the *hope* of transformation, of the coming of justice, mercy and peace. If Christianity in its former heartlands is to recover credibility it is imperative that it hears the cries of the members of the body of Christ across the Majority World, and responds to them in solidarity, growing militancy and in its own recovery of the biblical tradition of the prayer of lament as a core part of its worship and spirituality. My hope and prayer is that this book might make a small contribution toward that end.

I must once again request the indulgence of professional scholars in the various disciplines into which I have ventured in writing this book. I am not a professional biblical scholar, nor an academic theologian, and even less am I trained as a historian or a sociologist, but I have drawn valuable insights and offered comment in all of these areas. If in so doing I have made mistakes I would request my critics to recognize that my motivation was the quest for a deeper understanding of contemporary reality as the prerequisite for a more faithful Christian praxis at a critical period in human history.

Finally, I must thank a host of people who have encouraged me in pursuing this project. When it became known that I was attempting to write a book on this theme I received huge support online from friends, former students and complete strangers, all urging me to persist with this writing and bring the book to birth. I am deeply grateful to people far too numerous to mention who posted messages of support and whose words suggested that there is, indeed, a deep hunger out there for honesty concerning suffering, doubt and the perceived silences of God. In particular, Elizabeth Swain read my early chapters and made helpful comment; Wes White, as ever, has been a rock to me, urging me on while also allowing me the benefit of his critical insights; and I must single out Jim Gordon who offered me a comment at a critical moment in this writing which helped me more than he could ever know.

At another critical point in my writing Jenni and Andrew Green offered me generous hospitality in their beautiful farmhouse in a remote location in the Scottish Borders; the warmth of their fellowship combined with their prayerful concern for this project resulted in a mental logjam being broken and significant progress being made toward the completion of the book. I cannot thank them enough. I am very grateful to Alistair Wilson and his students at Edinburgh Theological Seminary for inviting me to share the outline of this work at one of their postgraduate seminars, and for the most stimulating and encouraging feedback I received on that occasion. During the final stages of writing this book I engaged in a dialogue with my friend and colleague Vinoth Ramachandra in which we shared each other's burdens and discussed the problem posed to our faith by the experience of suffering and personal loss. Those conversations were a high privilege for me and that this book should now be commended by Vinoth, whose own work and ministry has long been a source of inspiration, is both humbling and encouraging. I must also thank the staff at Langham Publishing, especially Pieter Kwant and Vivian Doub, for their help and support in bringing this book to birth. They have been efficient and patient, often going the extra mile in dealing with an author who delayed responding to their questions. It is a pleasure to work with such a publisher.

Two other people have played major supporting roles in the completion of this book: Michael Manning, with both written encouragement and the inspiration I gain from his remarkable example of faithfulness in discipleship on the Isle of Man, has given me the courage to press on, and Siobhan Wheeler repeatedly blessed me with both generous feedback and honest criticism. Siobhan played a big part in getting this work across the line. *Go raibh mile maith agat.*

David Smith
Glasgow, January 2020

1

Recovering a Lost Biblical Tradition

In 1981 Professor Robert Davidson delivered a series of lectures at the University of Glasgow which were subsequently published under the title *The Courage to Doubt: Exploring an Old Testament Theme.*[1] Attracted by the unusual title, I obtained a copy of this book soon after I had commenced studies at the University of Aberdeen, having returned from missionary service in the rainforests of Eastern Nigeria with a host of questions triggered by the challenges of living and teaching in a cross-cultural context. My questions related to cultural issues, but also to ethical concerns arising from exposure to the reality of the yawning gulf between the access to wealth and opportunity in the modern Western world and the poverty, disease and lack of medical resources in a traditional setting in Nigeria. Although living close to what would then have been called a "bush area," I had spent time in Nigeria's burgeoning cities, including Kaduna and Kano in the Muslim north and Calabar and Port Harcourt in the south, but the decisive, life-changing experience was in the sprawling, confusing, yet vibrant capital city of Lagos. There for the first time I encountered the African slum at its most extreme and was left stunned by the conditions I had witnessed, while almost equally amazed at the discovery of faith and hope of a kind never encountered previously in my life.

Consequently, I arrived in Aberdeen to commence a Religious Studies degree with a deeply personal agenda and a sense of great urgency in relation to the questions emerging from the experience of post-colonial Africa. This urgency was compounded by the growing realization that my theology appeared to be incapable of coping with the issues which so disturbed me. The

---

1. Robert Davidson, *The Courage to Doubt: Exploring an Old Testament Theme* (London: SCM, 1983).

questions simply lay beyond the scope of the theology I had taken to Nigeria and which, indeed, I had preached for more than a decade in the university city of Cambridge. Many of my certainties had begun to display signs of serious stress on the five-week voyage on a Nigerian cargo ship which commenced our African pilgrimage, but as the years passed and understanding of this new world deepened, I came to the conclusion that, despite having exercised an expository Bible teaching ministry for more than eleven years, I must have somehow missed something really crucial in my understanding of Scripture and of the biblical faith. Alternatively, if that were not the case, I was faced with the disturbing possibility that that faith itself offered no way of responding to the realities of a broken and suffering world, in which case I would have to ask whether my whole life had been based on an illusion.

It becomes clear why, in this context, Davidson's title drew my attention like a magnet. I had indeed been wrestling with doubt; how could my version of the gospel come as good news in a situation where life expectancy was so low and I had to provide transport for the corpse of a young man who had died as the result of the lack of medical services capable of responding to preventable diseases? More particularly, given my theological background, how could I relate the version of the Calvinist doctrine of divine predestination and providence which I had imbibed, a doctrine which resulted in a spirituality of unquestioning submission to the divine will even when it appeared profoundly mysterious and involved unbearable suffering, to the human pain and oppression which I had now encountered?

Davidson's book drew attention to the tradition of *lament* in the Old Testament and I can still recall my sense of relief and gratitude when I read these words in his first chapter: "In every age faith involved a struggle, a struggle to understand the ways of God whose presence was celebrated in worship, but who often seemed strangely absent. 'Why?' and 'How long?' were repeatedly discovered to be as authentic cries as 'Hallelujah.'"[2]

Davidson went on to demonstrate the truth of this claim through a careful study of the Hebrew Bible, examining the language of *lament* in worship as this is found again and again in the Psalms but also in the narratives of communal and individual histories, most notably in the case of Jeremiah. He commented that the courageous *public* preaching of the prophet and his strikingly honest confession of *private* anguish demonstrate that "outward courage and assurance are compatible with inner turmoil and doubt." Although I had long been aware of the language of lament in the Bible, not least because I had preached

---

2. Davidson, *Courage to Doubt*, 12.

many sermons on these very texts, it had not truly registered with me. The combination of a theological system which closed off certain questions and so prevented deep listening to the message of the Bible, and life experience remote from the suffering, abuse and violence known to Israel's prophets, had screened out of my consciousness the reality of the extent of conflict in the life of faith and the anguished questions to which this could give rise. Now, with the issues brought back from sub-Saharan Africa burning in my soul and the insights of a careful exegete enlarging my understanding, these familiar texts began to *explode* with previously unknown relevance at both a personal and a public level.[3]

What do I mean by the public dimension? People who spend a significant amount of time living in another culture from that within which they were nurtured and socialized not only confront the challenge of adjustment to that new context, but at a later stage are likely to re-enter their own cultural world, only to discover that this now presents a new and different set of challenges. This has sometimes been described as "reverse culture shock," since the person now coming "home" is no longer the same person who had left familiar shores years earlier, and, in addition, the culture to which that person now returns may have changed in significant and disturbing ways. The new lenses which are the gift of cross-cultural life and experience result in fresh perspectives on the world as a whole and on one's own culture in particular, but they thereby create distance, and possibly dissonance, between the returning exile and friends and family who have remained embedded within the familiar world that is "home." The desperate, life-and-death urgency of the questions with which I was wrestling was not – could not be – understood by people I loved and cared for, and a similar sense of detachment occurred in relationships with the wider Christian community. How could that community appear to be so relentlessly *happy* and untroubled in a world filled with injustice, oppression and violence? And (forgetting my own previous ignorance) why could they not see the importance of being honest about the glaring reality of the inequalities

---

3. The language of prophetic texts "exploding" recalls the work of Walter Brueggemann which was to be hugely important for me at a later stage. He discusses the way in which prophetic texts *linger* when written down and preserved as Scripture, only to *explode* at a later date when a particular set of life circumstances causes them to come alive with new power and relevance. Brueggemann says that such explosions depend upon "a capacity for imagination and intuition, coupled with courage, which dares to assert that these texts, concretely located and specifically addressed, can now be and must be concretely relocated and specifically readdressed as illuminating and revelatory in contemporary contexts." *Texts That Linger, Words That Explode* (Minneapolis: Fortress, 2000), 18.

of our times, of the tragedies unfolding among millions of our brothers and sisters, and of the issues this situation raised for faith?

It seems that cross-cultural life is one of those human experiences (there are others to which I will return later) which create a new and deeper sensitivity to human suffering and give birth to a new depth of compassion for people who live on the margins of the world, whether in post-colonial Africa or among the underclass of the capitalist societies of the Global North. Having returned from the former, I now had to try to understand what had happened during my absence in the latter, and to come to terms with a cultural world which seemed to have changed almost beyond recognition. In addition I was now entering the rarefied atmosphere of academia and here I found to my surprise that many people who were alienated from institutional Christianity were asking profound questions about the meaning of human existence and the source of love and justice. In other words, I now moved among honest *doubters* who had lost faith, yet acknowledged with surprising candour the aching heart and the deep existential questions which arose from within their own worldviews. It was this context which made me appreciate the *public* relevance of the biblical tradition of lament.

As a Scottish Presbyterian, Robert Davidson noticed that almost all traces of lament had disappeared from the public worship of the churches within his own tradition. At some point in the twentieth century, while psalm-singing was retained in the Church of Scotland, the psalms of lament were edited out of hymn books. Davidson quoted the German scholar Claus Westermann as saying that the lament had been excluded from Western Christianity "with the result that it has completely disappeared above all from prayer and worship." In a pioneering study of the Psalms, Westermann wrote that it is an illusion to suppose that

> there can be a relationship with God in which there was only praise and never lamentation. Just as joy and sorrow in alternation are part of the finitude of human existence (Gen 2–3), so praise and lamentation are part of man's relationship to God. Hence, something must be amiss if praise of God has a place in Christian worship but lamentation does not. *Praise can retain its authenticity and naturalness only in polarity with lamentation.*[4]

---

4. Claus Westermann, *Praise and Lament in the Psalms*, 2nd ed. (Atlanta: John Knox, 1981), 267; emphasis added. See also his *Living Psalms* (Grand Rapids, MI: Eerdmans, 1989). Walter Brueggemann has published extensively on the Psalms, including *Israel's Praise: Doxology against Idolatry and Ideology* (Philadelphia: Fortress, 1988); *Abiding Astonishment: Psalms, Modernity,*

What makes this strange mutation in the patterns of worship in Western Christianity so odd and tragic is that it happened at a time when modern historians were describing the twentieth century as "the age of catastrophe."[5] As we shall see, the most profound of all the laments in the Bible arose from the ruins of a destroyed city in the immediate aftermath of unspeakable violence and barbarity, which only increases our amazement that such prayers should have disappeared from the churches in a century in which not just a few cities were devastated, but urban centres across Europe were laid waste with civilian casualties on an unprecedented scale. Tony Judt observes that the number of people killed during the Second World War "dwarfs the mortality figures for the Great War of 1914–1918, obscene as those were," and goes on to point out that at least nineteen million of those deaths were of non-combatant civilians.[6] Little wonder that the musician Yehudi Menuhin spoke for many who lived through this period when he said, "If I had to sum up the twentieth century, I would say that it raised the greatest hopes ever conceived by humanity, and destroyed all illusions and ideals."[7] In precisely this *public* context, Davidson's questions resonate in a very powerful manner:

> Is . . . the tradition of faith in which we are nurtured so radically different from that of the psalmist that this is an element of Israel's hymn book to which, in the light of Christ, the Christian says an emphatic "no"? Why then is it that it is the words of just such a lament that we find on the lips of Jesus on the cross? Why is it that there are many people in the church today who seem near

---

and the Making of History (Louisville: Westminster John Knox, 1991); and *Spirituality of the Psalms* (Minneapolis: Fortress, 2002).

5. This phrase is used by Eric Hobsbawm to describe the first half of the twentieth century. See his *Age of Extremes: The Short Twentieth Century, 1914–1991* (London: Abacus, 1995). See also Tony Judt, *Postwar: A History of Europe since 1945* (London: Vintage, 2010); Timothy Snyder, *Bloodlands: Europe between Hitler and Stalin* (London: Vintage, 2011); and Mark Mazower, *Dark Continent: Europe's Twentieth Century* (London: Penguin, 1998).

6. Judt, *Postwar*, 18. It is difficult to take in the details which Judt chronicles, yet one of the characteristics of the lament tradition is that it spells out the reality of catastrophe in all its terrible dimensions, thus naming the horror which has created such a spiritual crisis. The British experience of the Second World War is familiar to many readers, but consider: the military losses of the Soviet Union amounted to 8.6 million soldiers; 5.5 million were taken prisoner by the Germans, of which 3.3 million died of starvation and mistreatment. In Vienna 87,000 women were raped by Soviet soldiers in three weeks following the Russian arrival; in Berlin there were 53,000 lost children by the end of the war; while in Rome thousands of mutilated, disfigured and unclaimed children huddled in the Quirinale Gardens. How could the lament tradition of the Bible go missing in a world like this?

7. Yehudi Menuhin quoted in Eric Hobsbawm, *Age of Extremes: The Short Twentieth Century, 1914–1991* (London: Abacus, 1995), 2.

to the psalmists in their need, people who have radical doubts about some of the traditional certainties, people crushed by the bitter reality of evil in their lives, people who find it far from easy to affirm the living presence of God in their experience, people who have long since ceased to pray since their prayers seem to go out into an unanswering silence, people who are asking in terms of our age the same questions that haunted the psalmists "why?" and "how long?"[8]

As I write these lines it is now well over thirty years since I discovered Robert Davidson's book. Pulling it down from my shelves I found a handwritten letter from him, a response to my communication expressing gratitude for his work. He indicated that feedback on his writing had been very encouraging with many readers expressing gratitude, "not least some on the fringe who needed to be reassured that a mature faith was not inconsistent with wrestling honestly with difficult questions."

Much has changed in the intervening years, but in the postmodern, globalized world in which we now find ourselves the need for the honesty and integrity of faith found on the pages of the Old Testament is greater than ever. Yet, in that same period, the biblical tradition of lament has receded ever further from the worshipping and devotional life of the churches in the West, lost and largely forgotten as the onrushing tide of postmodernism has left us with new forms of Christianity which focus almost exclusively on celebration and victory and appear to interpret the gospel as a kind of therapy for the satisfaction of personal needs and desires. Beyond, and very likely *within*, this distinctively contemporary form of religion there remain aching hearts and a host of people in an ever-increasing fringe who have profound and important questions and who must either suppress these in order to retain credibility within the believing community or turn elsewhere in the quest for sympathetic and understanding listeners who will take their sense of the *ambiguities* of faith seriously.

I have written this book in part because I have felt the compulsion to bear personal testimony to the fact that faith is strengthened and matured precisely through openness and honesty concerning doubt and difficulty. At the same time, I want to insist that a questioning, honest faith is exactly what we find in the Bible, and that this is the normal pathway to spiritual maturity. The prayer of lament is neither marginal within the biblical tradition, nor is it superseded in the New Testament, left behind as an archaic form of Jewish religion once

---

8. Davidson, *Courage to Doubt*, 15–16.

the light of the world has shone upon us. This seems to be the assumption made by many Christians, as though the light shining from the empty tomb on Easter Sunday morning obliterates even the memory of the horror of Good Friday and Holy Saturday and renders the language of the psalms of lament not only redundant, but actually inadmissible as a form of Christian prayer and spirituality.[9] I hope to show that this view, whether articulated verbally or simply taken for granted with minimal reflection, not only betrays a serious misunderstanding of the Hebrew Bible, but also fails to recognize the struggles and ambiguities of faith which are clearly present in the gospels and elsewhere in the New Testament.

I began this chapter by referring to the life-transforming impact of the experience of living in an African cultural context. I have described how this resulted in a re-reading of the Bible and the discovery of neglected texts which validated the struggle with difficult questions and revealed how, far from being a negative thing, wrestling with honest doubt is part and parcel of a genuine Christian spirituality and can stimulate progress on the path toward a mature faith. However, I must add that in subsequent years, having spent much time in different parts of Africa and Asia, I have come to realize that the neglect of the traditions of lament by Christians in the Western world is not replicated across the Majority World, where millions of members of the body of Christ live in circumstances which mean that those very traditions *are crucial to spiritual survival in an unjust and cruel world.* We will discuss specific examples of non-Western appreciation and use of the lament tradition elsewhere in this book, but I notice here the testimony of the Hispanic-American theologian Justo González, who describes how huge numbers of Christians have migrated from their own countries and understand very well what it means to be *a people in exile.* Like those ancient Jewish exiles who "sat and wept" beside the rivers of Babylon, Christians living in strange lands, with traumatic memories of their devastated homes, or reliving the terrible journeys endured in the quest for safety, cannot exist without the biblical tradition of the lament.

---

9. Leslie C. Allen, in what is a very moving and unusual exposition of the book of Lamentations, claims that "there is no obvious New Testament parallel to its theological interpretation of the fall of Jerusalem in 586 BCE as the wholesale punishment of the people by an angry God for their sins." Lamentations, he says, should "not be directly taken over by Christian readers" and its "pre-Christian content has to be read with theological sensitivity." *A Liturgy of Grief: A Pastoral Commentary on Lamentations* (Grand Rapids, MI: Baker Academic, 2011), 28–29. I understand the point Allen is making, but I think he exaggerates the difference between the Hebrew Bible and the New Testament and ignores the fact that Jerusalem was once again destroyed in 70 CE, an event so terrible that some have regarded it as similar to the Holocaust of the twentieth century. Furthermore, a large section of the New Testament was written in the aftermath of this world-shattering event *and reflects this context.*

By the waters of Babylon we shall live and die. By the waters of Babylon we shall sing the songs of Zion. Our Zion is not in the lands where we were born, though we still love them, for those lands are lost to us forever – and, in any case, since we have lived for a long time beyond innocence, we could never equate those lands with Zion. The Zion to which we sing, the Zion toward which we live, is the coming order of God, where all will have a vine and a fig tree under which to sit, and *none shall make them afraid* (Micah 4:4). And while we wait for that day, it may be that, as exiles, we have some insights into what it means to be a pilgrim people of God, followers of the One who had nowhere to lay his head.[10]

---

10. Justo L. González, *Mañana: Christian Theology from a Hispanic Perspective* (Nashville: Abingdon Press, 1990), 42.

For Reflection

> Why does the Almighty not set times for judgement?
> > Why must those who know him look in vain for such days?
> Men move boundary stones;
> > they pasture flocks they have stolen.
> They drive away the orphan's donkey
> > and take the widow's ox in pledge.
> They thrust the needy from the path
> > and force all the poor of the land into hiding.
> Like wild donkeys in the desert,
> > the poor go about their labour of foraging food;
> > the wasteland provides food for their children.
> They gather fodder in the fields
> > and glean in the vineyards of the wicked.
> Lacking clothes, they spend the night naked;
> > they have nothing to cover themselves in the cold.
> They are drenched by mountain rains
> > and hug the rocks for lack of shelter.
> The fatherless child is snatched from the breast;
> > the infant of the poor is seized for a debt.
> Lacking clothes, they go about naked;
> > they carry the sheaves, but still go hungry.
> They crush olives among the terraces;
> > they tread the winepresses, yet suffer thirst.
> The groans of the dying rise from the city,
> > and the souls of the wounded cry out for help.
> But God charges no-one with wrongdoing. (Job 24:1–12)

The problem of speaking correctly about God amid unjust suffering is not limited to the case of Job, but is a challenge to every believer. This is especially true of situations in which the suffering reaches massive proportions.[11]

---

11. Gustavo Gutiérrez, *On Job: God-Talk and the Suffering of the Innocent* (Maryknoll: Orbis, 1987), 11.

2

The Testimony of Biblical Israel

We have heard Claus Westermann describe the relationship between praise and lament as a polarity; another way to express this is to say that the depiction of the struggles of faith in the Bible is so persistent and frequent as to create a *dialectic* between the confession of belief in the living and faithful God, which forms the very heart of the tradition, and the doubts which arise from circumstances which call that faith into question. No one, to my knowledge, has expressed this with greater clarity than Walter Brueggemann who takes nearly two hundred pages to describe "Israel's Core Testimony," the central affirmation by which this people bears witness to a God who is just and righteous, faithful and compassionate. Brueggemann concludes that the righteousness of the God of the Bible is the foundation of the promise and hope of the well-being of the world, since when that righteousness becomes a reality on the plane of human history, "the results are fruitfulness, prosperity, freedom, justice, peace, security, and well-being (*shalom*)."[1]

When it becomes a reality on the plane of history – but here we come up against the problem that history very often tells a different story in which the promise at the core of faith appears to be contradicted by events and the righteous God remains silent and apparently inactive. Thus, *within* Israel's faith tradition (not from outside it) there arises what Brueggemann describes as the "Countertestimony" in which those who confess their embrace of, and commitment to, the core beliefs are heard asking searching questions. These may be addressed to God in prayer or shared openly within the community of faith, but either way they concern the dissonance between what has been promised and is hoped for and the painful realities of historical and personal experiences which call aspects of the foundational beliefs into doubt. Brueggemann expresses this tension as follows:

---

1. Walter Brueggemann, *Theology of the Old Testament: Testimony, Dispute, Advocacy* (Minneapolis: Fortress, 1997), 303.

Israel's testimony to Yahweh has proposed a God who in majestic sovereignty provides a viable life-order in the world through decisive, transformative interventions, a God who in generous compassion attends to the needs of Yahweh's own. But Israel's lived experience appears to deliver neither viable life-order nor generous compassion – certainly not by highly visible, nameable acts of intervention.[2]

The counter-testimony of biblical Israel is expressed both by individuals in personal distress and despair and by the community as a whole at those points at which something appears to have gone seriously adrift with history. We will look at examples in both of these categories below, but first, notice that the lament is embedded in the very foundations of Israel's faith in that cries of anguish on the part of oppressed and despairing slaves are described as the trigger for the event of liberation and redemption which created this people and gave them both a hope and a mission. According to Exodus 3:7–9, God heard the cries of the slaves in Egypt and declared, "I am concerned about their suffering . . . [and] the way the Egyptians are oppressing them." This event, with the pattern of a cry to heaven in a hopeless situation and the response of the righteous Lord in an act of deliverance which brings about complete transformation, comes to be recalled as belonging to the very core of the tradition: "But the Egyptians ill-treated us and made us suffer, putting us to hard labour. *Then we cried out to the LORD, the God of our fathers, and the LORD heard our voice and saw our misery, toil and oppression*" (Deut 26:6–7).[3] On the basis of these texts Claus Westermann concludes, "In the Old Testament, from beginning to end, the 'call of distress,' the 'cry out of the depths,' that is, the lament, is an inevitable part of what happens between God and man."[4]

What Has Job Ever Done for Us?

In February 2017 I travelled to Pakistan to visit a former student of mine. He had indicated that he would like me to teach in Lahore and Karachi and contribute to a conference of pastors in the interior of the Province of Sindh. Months before this journey I read everything I could find on Pakistan, especially regarding the situation in Sindh. I learned a great deal concerning

---

2. Brueggemann, *Theology of the Old Testament*, 318.

3. All emphasis in Scripture quotes has been added.

4. Westermann, *Praise and Lament*, 261.

the influence of Sufi Islam in this area and how its tolerance of local cultural practices involving the veneration of the shrines of saints and festivals at which crowds of men and women danced in celebration of those whose lives they revered, practices which reached back into the ancient Hindu past, aroused the suspicion of other Muslims and resulted in violent attempts to suppress such customs. In fact, the week before I was due to travel to Pakistan, fundamentalists supporting the Islamic State sent a suicide bomber on a mission of death amid a crowd of Sufi dancers in Sindh, killing almost ninety people. In addition to the threat of violence, I also discovered that rural people suffered from extreme poverty and that low-caste Hindu villagers close to the border with India faced serious oppression as, according to Anatol Lieven, "Sindhi landowners and tribal chieftains dominate the province and milk Karachi's economy for their own benefit."[5]

The day I arrived in Sindh I found myself sitting beside a retired teacher who responded to my questions concerning what I had read about the local situation with heart-rending accounts of the oppression of villagers by powerful landowners who mistreated and abused the day labourers who tilled their fields. Later, I was taken to one such remote village, a tiny settlement in the middle of nowhere, and witnessed the pathetic condition of one of these communities. Yet here, as in the slums of Lagos years earlier, I discovered yet again a richness of faith and generosity of spirit which reduced me to tears and left me with images of the kindness of the poor which will remain with me for the rest of my life.

However, I also faced a huge dilemma: *what on earth did I have to offer the assembly of poor pastors, many of whom came from villages like the one I had just visited, when we met together the next morning?* My pre-reading had driven me to the conviction that the only possibility of speaking into this situation with some degree of credibility was provided by a serious and sustained reflection on the message of the book of Job. This classic statement of the Old Testament wisdom tradition, in which the lament may be said to reach its apogee, has been largely neglected in the theology of Christian mission since it cannot be easily incorporated within a "grand narrative" of progress, advance and success.[6] Indeed, in the book of Job the counter-testimony of

---

5. Anatol Lieven, *Pakistan: A Hard Country* (London: Penguin, 2002), 317.

6. Christopher Wright's *The Mission of God: Unlocking the Bible's Grand Narrative* (Downers Grove, IL: InterVarsity Press, 2006) makes only passing reference to Job, despite being largely focused on the Old Testament. However, he does discuss the wisdom tradition in general and helpfully comments that its presence within the Bible should "compel us toward an honest faith that is willing to acknowledge the existence of doubts we cannot entirely dismiss and questions

biblical Israel finds its clearest and boldest expression, presenting a challenge to God's silence and absence in the face of the extremes of human suffering in statements which must appear shocking to a piety which knows only the language of praise and submission.

The story of Job is well known and has repeatedly attracted the interest of artists, musicians and writers who have recognized it as wrestling in a most dramatic manner with the universal problem of human suffering. Indeed, Job-like figures show up in stories told across the ancient Near East, so that this book has an international feel about it which makes its message relevant and powerful in contexts of deep distress far beyond the limits of biblical Israel. Job's own suffering is extreme; the narrator ratchets up the tension in describing how this honoured and god-fearing man was plunged into the deepest depths of humiliation and despair by a succession of tragedies involving death and destruction, economic disaster and the collapse of his own health. His friends, who are to play a central part in the dialogues which follow, are unable to recognize Job, and at the horrifying sight of the shell of the person they once knew they weep aloud and sit with him in wordless sympathy for seven days: "No-one said a word to him, because they saw how great his suffering was" (Job 2:13). Alas, this silence was soon to be forgotten as, in response to Job's anguished cries, cursing the day of his birth, a veritable torrent of words is unleashed.

Two particular aspects of this complex and lengthy book have become very significant to me, one of which connects powerfully to the plight of those pastors I addressed in the Pakistani Sindh, while the other relates to my own pilgrimage and the spiritual and theological questions it has raised. The book describes the *external* reality of the tragic events which devastated Job's life and laid him low. But it then proceeds to bring to the surface the *private and internal* anguish which is the inevitable result of such tragedies, yet often goes unrecognized and unnoticed. This is the phenomenon we have come to describe as *trauma*, the deep internal wounding of the spirit and the emotions as the pain of loss undermines previously secure and stable beliefs and can drive the sufferer to the brink of a precipice of despair and meaninglessness. As the shell-shocked friends react to the violence of Job's language, he makes a statement which needs to be heard by Christians who imagine either that it is possible to sing one's way out of depression or that the mere repetition of dogmatic certainties is enough to subdue the sufferer's doubts: "A despairing

---

we cannot satisfactorily answer within the limits of our experience or even the limits of the revelation God has chosen to give us" (450).

man should have the devotion of his friends, even though he forsakes the fear of the Almighty" (6:14).

However, as the dialogues proceed and Job becomes increasingly alienated from his friends and their dogmatic theology, he reveals a growing awareness of, and sensitivity to, the pain and despair of other human beings who have only ever known lives marked by oppression and injustice. He speaks of "poor country people" who "have to keep out of sight," and who "go about naked . . . [and] hungry" as they work the fields of the rich landowners (24:1–12).[7] *The language used here resonated with the villagers in the Pakistani Sindh since the description of the distress and despair of humble people in biblical times exactly mirrored their experience in the twenty-first century.*

However, as Job laments God's failure to judge those responsible for such inhuman oppression, he also recognizes that the evil and injustice he witnesses within society *has human causes*. Gustavo Gutiérrez detects a change in the tone of Job's language as he discovers that poverty and abandonment

> are not something fated but are caused by the wicked who nonetheless live serene and satisfied lives. The poverty described is not the result of destiny or inexplicable causes; those responsible for it are named without pity. Job is describing a state of affairs caused by the wickedness of those who exploit and rob the poor. In many instances therefore, the suffering of the innocent points clearly to guilty parties.[8]

So how does God fit into this picture? In the final section of the book God appears and subjects Job to a series of questions, culminating in the statement that if the sufferer really believes that he possesses the wisdom and power to govern the world in all its complexity, mystery and brokenness, then God will admit "that your own right hand can save you" (40:14).[9] In other words, God will retreat from history and allow human beings to take full control of the world of creation and of human society. Suddenly this book becomes remarkably contemporary in a context in which modern people no longer

---

7. Gutiérrez, *On Job*, 33.

8. Gutiérrez, 32–33.

9. Note the perceptive comment of Gerald Janzen that Job's charge against divine justice presumes that "the perfect reign (or royal rule) of order and justice would exemplify irresistible exercise of unilateral power, imposed 'from the top down,' a vision the totalitarian character of which should not be less odious for being projected upon God." By contrast, the message of the book is that "true royalty engages 'proud' power otherwise than by brute force." J. Gerald Janzen, *Job*, Interpretation: A Bible Commentary for Teaching and Preaching (Atlanta: John Knox, 1985), 244.

flinch from accepting this challenge and actually celebrate the death of God as an opportunity for human beings to take complete responsibility for the governance of life on earth in all its dimensions.[10]

While Job shows his embrace of the covenantal tradition as he shrinks back from such a possibility and confesses that his language had been unwise, the fact remains that the book implies that the question of theodicy requires a response from God. And that response is forthcoming in the shape of the explicit rejection of the friends' theology and their arraignment for "not [having] spoken of me what is right, as my servant Job has" (42:7–8). Here is the point at which the message of this extraordinary book suddenly appeared to connect with my personal concerns described in the previous chapter. God's repudiation of the standard wisdom tradition as this had hardened into a rigid cause-and-effect theology, and his even more remarkable vindication of Job's theological questing, *suggests a divine self-questioning and previously unrecognized depths in the Lord's own struggle to control the powers of evil and bring about the promised healing of the broken world.* Indeed, this crucial revelation of the divine character expands and enlarges upon a statement found at the very beginning of the book in which *God is confronted by the crucial question of the real motivation of human worship and devotion* (1:9–11).[11]

In 1946, as the cities of Hiroshima and Nagasaki lay in ruins and the Japanese people were numbed by the outcome of war and the extent of the devastation and death visited upon them, a theologian previously unknown outside Asia named Kazoh Kitamori published a book with the title *Theology of the Pain of God.* I suspect that he had no knowledge of the poignant words of a fellow Christian in Germany who, a little more than a year earlier while awaiting execution by the Nazis, had written that amid the chaos and

---

10. See Yuval Noah Harari's book *Homo Deus: A Brief History of Tomorrow* (London: Vintage, 2017). Translated into forty languages worldwide this has become a publishing phenomenon. Unlike Job this writer has no doubts about the human ability to replace God: "Having secured unprecedented levels of prosperity, health and harmony, and given our past record and present values, humanity's next targets are likely to be immortality, happiness and divinity. . . . And having raised humanity above the beastly level of survival struggles, we will now aim to upgrade humans into gods, and turn *Homo sapiens* into *Homo Deus*" (24).

11. Gerald Janzen says in the introduction to his commentary on Job that the human question concerning the meaning of suffering is inseparable from "the divine question as to the motivation and character, and therefore the meaning, of human piety and rectitude." In confronting and responding to both of these questions "the book of Job may be seen as contributing to a deepening of the bases, a re-casting of the nature, and a renewal of the viability of the divine–human covenant relation." *Job*, 20–21.

devastation of global war, "Only a suffering God can help."[12] Kitamori's book developed a very closely related theme:

> God in the gospel is the One who resolves our pain and the Lord who heals our wounds. This means that he is our "Savior." What is salvation? Salvation is the message that our God enfolds our broken reality. A God who embraces us completely – this is God our Savior. Is there a more astonishing miracle in the world than that God embraces our broken reality? Our reality is utterly and hopelessly broken. Yet the gospel brings us the message of "hope even for the hopeless" – yea, rather, "hope *only* for the hopeless." Those who believe this gospel believe against their own hope (Rom. 4:18). This all-embracing God resolves our pain and heals our wounds. Accordingly, the pain of God which resolves our pain is "love" rooted in his pain.[13]

Kitamori found the evidence of the "pain of God" in the incarnation and death of the crucified Messiah, but that divine embrace of our "broken reality" is already anticipated in the narrative of Job which bears testimony to the price which God must pay to bring his promised *shalom* to a world of injustice, rebellion and suffering.

The Crisis of Faith at Ground Zero

If the book of Job reveals the depths of the spiritual crisis which can arise for an *individual* in the face of unbearable personal suffering, Lamentations reflects the impact of a terrible catastrophe which has overwhelmed an entire *community*. In this respect, these two neglected biblical books parallel the distinction between personal and communal laments in the book of Psalms. Indeed, the historical event which gave birth to the outpouring of grief in Lamentations is also the context in which the psalmists describe how an invading army had "given the dead bodies of your servants as food to the

---

12. This famous phrase was, of course, penned by Dietrich Bonhoeffer. Here it is in context: "God allows himself to be edged out of the world and on to the cross. God is weak and powerless in the world, and that is exactly the way, the only way, in which he can be with us and help us. Matthew 8:17 makes it crystal clear that it is not by his omnipotence that Christ helps us, but by his weakness and suffering. . . . Man's religiosity makes him look in his distress to the power of God in the world. . . . The Bible however directs him to the powerlessness and suffering of God; *only a suffering God can help.*" Dietrich Bonhoeffer, *Letters and Papers from Prison* (London: Fontana, 1959), 122.

13. Kazoh Kitamori, *Theology of the Pain of God* (London: SCM, 1966), 20–21.

birds of the air" and "poured out blood like water all around Jerusalem, and there is no-one to bury the dead" (Ps 79:2–3). If those words focus attention upon the physical, psychological and mental impact of the terrible violence of ancient warfare, the writer of Psalm 74 is concerned with the *spiritual* consequences of the same disaster and the sense of abandonment, loneliness, and a complete loss of bearings which resulted from it: "We are given no miraculous signs; no prophets are left, *and none of us knows how long this will be*" (74:9). The language testifies to a kind of spiritual vertigo in which the shaking of foundational beliefs creates a sense of falling in a space with no up or down; drifting in a world now devoid of all the long-established structures which gave meaning, direction and hope to the shared life of the community. In addition, Psalm 74 highlights what is a central and constantly repeated concern for the author of Lamentations: *the terrible silence of heaven and the absence of a divine response or explanation.*

In fact, this silence is movingly reflected in the repeated cry of the desolate survivors of the destruction of Jerusalem in Lamentations that *there is no one to comfort me* (see Lam 1:9, 16, 21; 2:9; 3:8, 44). This absence of a source of comfort amid distress is very similar to the condition which we have come to describe as post-traumatic stress, but in this biblical book it both has a specifically spiritual dimension and reflects a shared, *communal* experience. The silence of God is reflected in the fact that prophets "no longer find visions from the LORD" (2:9). Jeremiah, whose words had cut through the hypocrisy and deceit of the kings and priests who maintained an insane optimism even in the final days of Jerusalem, had gone into exile in Egypt and with the silencing of his voice, genuine prophecy appeared to have come to a full stop. Worse still, God not only had become silent but also appeared to be *deaf*: "Even when I call out or cry for help, he shuts out my prayer" (3:8; see also v. 44). This is indeed the "dark night of the soul," but instead of being the testimony of a lonely, individual mystic, it is here the collective experience of a whole community enduring a shared loss of all the ties which had bound it together.

The relevance of this book in the context of the modern world has been well described by Kathleen O'Connor, who notes that "for survivors of civil wars, destroyed cities, and genocides, for refugees, and for those who subsist in famine and destitute poverty, the poetry mirrors reality with frightening exactitude."[14] The mention of "destroyed cities" in this list is particularly significant since Lamentations has been identified as belonging to a specific

---

14. Kathleen O'Connor, *Lamentations and the Tears of the World* (Maryknoll, NY: Orbis, 2002), 5.

class of laments arising from the deliberate targeting of ancient cities in warfare and their total destruction. Such "urban laments" are found throughout the ancient Near East, as the following lines from a poem lamenting the loss of the city of Ur illustrate:

> Large trees were being uprooted, the forest growth was ripped out,
> The orchards were being stripped of their fruit,
> They were being cleaned of their offshoots . . .
> . . . They piled up in heaps. . . . They spread out like sheaves.
> There were corpses [floating] in the Euphrates, brigands roamed
>   [the roads]
> The rich left his possessions and took an unfamiliar path. . . .
> Its king sat immobilized in the palace, all alone. . . .
> The palace of his delight, he was weeping bitterly.
> The devastating flood was levelling [everything],
> Like a great storm it roared over the earth, who could escape it?
> . . . Alas, the destroyed city, my destroyed temple. . . .
> On the fields fine grains grew not, people had nothing to eat.[15]

Of course, in addition to the death and suffering visited upon cities by military action (a reality now so common that modern scholars have invented the term "urbicide" to describe it), many urban communities in the twenty-first century face the destructive power of natural forces in the shape of floods, winds, earthquakes or volcanic eruptions. Billions of people now crowding into the burgeoning cities of Asia live beneath the shadow of the ever-present possibility of natural disasters and of rising sea levels capable of overwhelming the coastal megacities which now dot the landscape. Asia's geological configuration creates what has been described as "geographical conversations between lands and seas, highlands and lowlands, rivers and mountains." This context means that life is lived with "vulnerability, volatility and fragility" as constant companions, and "migrant workers, refugees of war and stateless peoples testify to the fragile and fluid conditions in human life

---

15. From Nancy C. Lee, *Lyrics of Lament: From Tragedy to Transformation* (Minneapolis: Fortress, 2010), 25. She comments: "No doubt, the powers that be across the nations in government, military, and media know that the airing of the voices of lament is dangerous and may unleash demands for change, or calls for an end to power always having its way at the expense of the powerless and often innocent masses, subjected to endless cycles of war, oppression, poverty and suffering" (24).

that are punctuated by the eruptions of wars, tsunamis and earthquakes."[16] As Michael Nai-Chiu Poon says, "Makeshift tents replace cathedrals as the carriers of Christianity at the start of the third millennium. Peoples are on the move; and so too faith is on the move. For many, life is apocalyptic. They live under the constant threat of an impending end."[17]

A specific example of what this means, and of the immediate theological and pastoral significance of the book of Lamentations in such a situation, is provided by the work of the Filipino scholar Federico Villanueva. His commentary on this book was written in the aftermath of the devastating impact of Typhoon Yolanda (Haiyan), the strongest such storm ever recorded, which left thousands dead and largely destroyed the coastal city of Tacloban in the Philippines. Villanueva describes how the centuries-long experience of the peoples of the Philippines of colonization, first under Spain, then at the hands of the Americans and Japanese, had created a culture of passivity accompanied by a sense of inferiority, so that for Filipino Christians a spirituality of lament was almost inconceivable. Yet when storm Yolanda swept through these islands, bringing death and destruction on an unprecedented scale, survivors found themselves spontaneously using language which unconsciously echoed that in the book of Lamentations, and this previously puzzling text suddenly became an indispensable pastoral resource for survival and eventual recovery. The once-distant deity who demanded unquestioning reverence and submission had to hear the anguished cries of the broken-hearted and submit to their interrogation, and Lamentations validated precisely this new relationship.

> God does not view us with contempt as our colonizers did. He does not want followers who only know how to say, "Yes, yes Lord." He sees us as covenant partners. Jesus calls us his friends, not his servants. He considers us co-workers in the vineyard (1 Cor. 3:9). God is not like some of our leaders who treat us like slaves and can never be questioned. He is not like a parent who tells us to shut up whenever we begin to open our mouth. The God of the Bible allows his servants to tell him what is on our hearts.[18]

---

16. Michael Nai-Chiu Poon, "The Rise of Asian Pacific Christianity and Challenges for the Church Universal," in *Ecumenical Visions for the 21st Century: A Reader for Theological Education*, ed. Mélisande Lorke and Dietrich Werner (Geneva: World Council of Churches, 2013), 69.

17. Poon, "Rise of Asian Pacific Christianity," 69.

18. Federico Villanueva, *Lamentations: A Pastoral and Contextual Commentary* (Carlisle: Langham Global Library, 2016), 14.

If centuries of colonial rule resulted in a passive and submissive form of spirituality in the Asian context just mentioned, what shall we say of the culture of the modern Western world which has produced a similar alienation from the lament tradition of the Bible, as we have already noted? Almost the only text in the book of Lamentations known to many Christians in Europe and North America is the sudden appearance of hope in chapter 3, with its declaration that God's "compassions never fail" and are "new every morning" (3:22–24). In the most bizarre fashion these words have been wrenched from their context, made the basis of a popular hymn and thus forced to justify a spirituality overflowing with joy, confidence and the untroubled assurance that the world is exactly as it should be:

> Pardon for sin, and a peace that endureth,
> Thine own dear presence to cheer and to guide;
> Strength for today and bright hope for tomorrow,
> Blessings all mine, with ten thousand beside.[19]

Whatever merits this composition may have when read without reference to the source of its opening lines, this is surely a dreadful misuse of Scripture, distorting the text from Lamentations by compelling it to serve an understanding of the life of faith completely at odds with the message of the book in which it is embedded. Why would Christians, especially those who hold a high view of the authority of the Bible, so blatantly distort the meaning of this text? The answer, I suspect, like the explanation of the Asian context discussed above, concerns *culture*; in this case it is not the culture of the colonized which must be examined, but that of the *colonizers* – the nations shaped by centuries of Christendom and possessed of the conviction that they are the bearers of truth and of a way of life destined to become universal. We cannot enlarge upon this culture here, except to say that an overweening confidence in progress and a conviction that Western civilization was the very embodiment of truth and justice resulted in a sense of global mission which left no space for lament.

There is a frightening analogy between this culture and that which the Hebrew prophets, especially Jeremiah, attacked as being a false ideology leading toward death! Walter Brueggemann has noticed how the grief of the prophets (their *lamenting* over Judah and Jerusalem) was treated as something odd and unpatriotic by

---

19. This is the final stanza of the hymn written by T. O. Chisholm which begins with the words "Great Is Thy Faithfulness."

the managers of the status quo who deceive themselves and others into pretending that there is no illness. They are fascinated with statistics. They are skilful at press conferences. They believe their own propaganda. They imagine that God loves rather than judges, that the Babylonian threat will soon disappear (cf. Jer. 28:2–4), that the economy is almost back to normal, that Judean values will somehow survive, that religion needs to be affirmative, that things will hold together if we all hug each other.[20]

We must add that the characteristics of modern culture which distance us from the lament tradition of the Bible also include the belief that science and technology will provide solutions to all human ills and lead us toward a world of ever-increasing human happiness. Consequently, as Robin Perry observes, we are "notoriously averse to pain and tragedy. We spend an extraordinary amount of money and effort seeking to insulate ourselves against life's vicissitudes." As a result, we have lost "a vocabulary of grief" and Lamentations "accosts us . . . as a stranger who offers us an unasked-for gift . . . the poetry of pain. *We would be wise to pay attention.*"[21]

It remains to ask how we might account for the sudden outburst of hope and praise at the centre of a book unremittingly focused on pain, loss and confusion. The great shaft of light which breaks into the pervading darkness of the lament comes at the very point at which the poetry reaches rock bottom:

> I have been deprived of peace;
>> I have forgotten what prosperity is.
> So I say, "My splendour is gone
>> and all that I had hoped from the LORD." (3:17–18)

Here is the point at which Israel's counter-testimony is articulated with the greatest clarity and with extraordinary boldness. And yet, it is at this precise moment that hope resurfaces: "Because of the LORD's great love we are not consumed, for his compassions never fail" (3:22). Is this not an anachronism which suggests that these verses may have been inserted by a later reader wanting to soften the blow of Lamentations?

I confess to having long been puzzled by this issue since the change of mood is so sudden, unexpected and extreme that it can appear artificial and unreal. However, I have come to see, both on the basis of personal experience

---

20. Walter Brueggemann, *Hopeful Imagination: Prophetic Voices in Exile* (Philadelphia: Fortress, 1986), 42.

21. Robin A. Parry, *Lamentations*, Two Horizons Old Testament Commentary (Grand Rapids, MI: Eerdmans, 2010), 1; emphasis added.

and through the testimonies of other people, that the sudden, unexpected shaft of light which bursts upon the sufferers is absolutely true to the reality of the lived experience of many men and women. The dawn breaks at the point at which the night is darkest, and the renewal of hope comes only after the lament for all that has been lost has done its necessary work and, through the shedding of tears, has opened a channel for life to be renewed in ways transcending the sufferers' imagining.

The eighteenth-century poet and hymn-writer William Cowper, who knew all too well the struggle with despair and grief, captures this reality in lines which were once regularly used in public worship but are now largely forgotten:

> Sometimes a light surprises
> The Christian while he sings;
> It is the Lord, who rises
> With healing in his wings;
> When comforts are declining,
> He grants the soul again
> A season of clear shining,
> To cheer it after rain.

Notice that Cowper connects the surprising appearance of the light and the renewal of hope with *music*; it is in the act of *singing* that the sufferer finds renewed joy. Leslie Allen has suggested that Lamentations "is best understood as the script for a *liturgy* intended as a therapeutic ritual" and that this service would have been performed amid the ruins of the Jerusalem temple.[22] Indeed, the language of 3:41 – "Let us lift up our hearts and hands to God in heaven ... " – does indeed suggest that at least sections of these poems may have been part of a public liturgy, and if so this must surely have included music. Elsewhere the Bible recognizes the crucial role of music more generally, and my own experience has been that this great gift can touch the broken heart in a manner both deeply mysterious and wonderful beyond rational explanation.

In the weeks and months after the passing of my dearest friend and partner in life, when I was utterly incapable of songs of praise and knew only a kind of emotional paralysis which drained life of joy and threatened the loss of meaning, I chanced upon a performance of Dmitri Shostakovich's fifteenth symphony which was the door for the renewal of personal hope. I cannot explain this; the music had previously been a puzzle I could not resolve, but on this occasion I understood the composer's language and the outpouring

---

22. Leslie C. Allen, *A Liturgy of Grief: A Pastoral Commentary on Lamentations* (Grand Rapids, MI: Baker Academic, 2011), 8–14.

of his own grief at a lifetime of intense suffering and now facing his own end, and heart spoke to heart as "the Lord rose with healing in his wings."

It becomes clear by this point, I trust, that the loss of the biblical tradition of lament is spiritually (perhaps also socially and politically) a disaster. The importance of being able to be honest to God is obvious in situations of extreme suffering involving events such as war, genocide and urbicide. But, as Kathleen O'Connor points out in her wonderful study of this text, in the prosperous and apparently secure societies of the Western world, "there are normal human losses to lament, deaths, disappointments, and hidden depression with which to contend." She writes of the situation in the United States, but her words apply more generally to the nations of the so-called developed world, that behind the external show of wealth and power "hide despair and a violent culture of denial that drains our humanity." For our own sakes "and for the sake of the world over which we try callously to preside, these things demand lamentation."[23]

The discussion above has described how major catastrophes can result in a crisis for faith which may often be shaken, or even undermined, by the experience of great suffering, but I end with the reminder that while faith may often be shaken, or even undermined, by the experience of great suffering, such disturbing experiences, often involving a close encounter with death and with previously unknown depths of evil and wickedness, can also provide the soil within which faith comes to birth. The apparent absence of God may result in counter-testimony on the part of the believing soul, but it can equally well stimulate a previously unknown quest for God as the inadequacy of a secular worldview is discovered in such a situation.

On 11 September 2001, Peter Heltzel was due to make his way to work in the World Financial Center in New York, but he was absent from his office on that day. When the Twin Towers were destroyed Heltzel was at home, left broken with his world literally destroyed. With other volunteers he went to Ground Zero in the following days "to work amidst the acrid smoke and the dust of souls lost that fateful day." He describes how rescue workers were united in despair, entering together "a collective dark night of the soul," and yet "It was there in Gehenna that I felt a call to work for a new future, a more just city and a new world."[24] The disaster of 9/11 was the context of a call to recognize the causes of such a tragedy and, in Peter Heltzel's words, "bear witness to God in *this* world through being actively engaged in a coalition of love and life."[25]

---

23. O'Connor, *Lamentations*, 5.

24. Peter Goodwin Heltzel, *Resurrection City: A Theology of Improvisation* (Grand Rapids, MI: Eerdmans, 2012), 6–7.

25. Heltzel, *Resurrection City*, 3.

For Reflection

How deserted lies the city,
  once so full of people!
How like a widow is she,
  who once was great among the nations!
She who was queen among the provinces
  has now become a slave.

Bitterly she weeps at night,
  tears are upon her cheeks.
Among all her lovers
  there is none to comfort her.
All her friends have betrayed her;
  they have become her enemies.

After affliction and harsh labour,
  Judah has gone into exile.
She dwells among the nations;
  she finds no resting place.
All who pursue her have overtaken her
  in the midst of her distress.

The roads to Zion mourn,
  for no-one comes to her appointed feasts.
All her gateways are desolate,
  her priests groan,
her maidens grieve,
  and she is in bitter anguish.

Her foes have become her masters;
  her enemies are at ease.
The LORD has brought her grief
  because of her many sins.
Her children have gone into exile,
  captive before the foe.

All the splendour has departed
  from the Daughter of Zion.
Her princes are like deer
  that find no pasture;
in weakness they have fled
  before the pursuer. . . .

"Is it nothing to you, all you who pass by?
    Look around and see.
Is any suffering like my suffering
    that was inflicted on me,
that the LORD brought on me
    in the day of his fierce anger? . . .

"This is why I weep
    and my eyes overflow with tears.
No-one is near to comfort me,
    no-one to restore my spirit.
My children are destitute
    because the enemy has prevailed." (Lam 1:1–6, 12, 16)

The Teufelsberg hill is comfortably the highest spot in Berlin. A large, verdant summit, it might easily be mistaken for a geological feature with a history stretching back millions of years. . . . And yet, Teufelsberg is barely fifty years old. Beneath its soils lie not a complex geological stratigraphy but the dark secrets of a verticalised total war. . . . one-seventh of all the rubble removed from the bombed-out cities of the whole of Germany [lies there]. . . . Much of the remains of pre-war Berlin, which totalled 50,000 burnt and bombed-out buildings . . . are piled high beneath the hill's surface . . . a dead city rests below a deceptively pastoral surface.[26]

---

26. Stephen Graham, *Vertical: The City from Satellites to Bunkers* (London: Verso, 2016), 281–282.

3

The Testimony of the Jesus Movement

In the previous two chapters we have seen how the prayer of lament is embedded within the faith and worship of biblical Israel from the beginning and that the dialectic between the confession of Yahweh's faithfulness, on the one hand, and doubts arising from experiences which seem to undermine such confidence, on the other, is present throughout the Hebrew Bible. The question which now confronts us is whether a similar pattern can be discerned within the New Testament, or is that dynamic now transcended by the life and work of Jesus Christ? Or, to put this more bluntly, does the announcement made by the gospel of the coming of Messiah, and with him the arrival of God's promised *shalom* and the fulfilment of all that the prophets had anticipated, place Christian believers in an entirely new situation within which the need for the prayer of lament is at least diminished, if not actually removed?

It is difficult to exaggerate the importance of this question. In those areas of the world which have for centuries constituted its heartlands, especially in Europe but increasingly in North America as well, Christianity is facing a crisis of such magnitude as to compel many serious observers to ask whether it can survive. Timothy Gorringe, for example, imagines a future in which historians will debate when and why "the terminal decline in Christianity" commenced, and he suggests they might conclude that dramatic advances in technology in the early third millennium finally completed the Enlightenment's work in overcoming superstition, while patriarchy, "which had been socially dominant since the inception of agriculture, finally gave way to new feminist forms of society, leaving the old patriarchal religions stranded."[1] Andrew Walls, in a

---

1. Timothy J. Gorringe, "After Christianity?," in *Christianity for the Twenty-First Century*, ed. Philip Essler (Edinburgh: T&T Clark, 1998), 261. Gorringe believes Christianity will survive, although in a radically transformed character. One of the reasons he gives for such a hope is

characteristically brilliant analysis, concludes that the failure of the churches in the West to call for repentance from the cult of Mammon and their pitiful accommodation of both worship and evangelism to the religion of consumerist individualism is evidence that Christianity in the West "ceased to have critical contact with Western culture" and could no longer "do it any harm or good."[2]

What these and many other studies suggest is that there is some kind of serious deformity in the message which the churches of the West have presented to the modern world, and while I would not want to suggest that the loss of the dimension of the biblical tradition discussed in this book constitutes the whole of the problem, it is, in my view, a significant part of it.[3] Seen from this perspective, the decline of Western Christianity, while involving much pain and anguish, can be viewed in a similar manner to the exile in Babylon, as a tragedy which conceals an unasked-for blessing, opening up entirely new spaces for repentance, recovery and renewal and so gifting us an opportunity to read the gospel with new lenses capable of overcoming our tragic blind spots.

Shalom and the Gospel of Peace

Tom Wright describes the cross of Jesus as "the moment when something *happened* as a result of which the world became a different place, inaugurating God's future plan." This was the day, he says, when "the revolution began," and the resurrection was proof positive that "it was indeed underway."[4] So what need have Christians of the prayer of lament? Do the books of Job and Lamentations, to say nothing of the Psalms and the prayers of Jeremiah, become of merely historical interest, without theological value with regard to Christian worship and spirituality? In practice, as we have seen, this is exactly

---

the "perception about power, violence and weakness to be found at its heart." The crucifixion of Jesus demonstrates that the weakness of God "is stronger than human understandings of power," which means that the God revealed in the gospel "is defined by the weakness of the cross and is not therefore the almighty tyrant of so much clerical fancy" (265).

2. Andrew Walls, "Christian Expansion and the Condition of Western Culture," Henry Martyn Lecture 1985 in *Changing the World* (Bromley: MARC Europe, n.d.), 23.

3. As already indicated the literature on this subject is vast and still growing. I have been challenged by Brad Gregory's *The Unintended Reformation: How a Religious Revolution Secularized Society* (Cambridge, MA: Belknap Press of Harvard University, 2012), especially ch. 5, "Manufacturing the Goods Life," 235–297. I have also learned much from Douglas John Hall's work, especially *The Cross in Our Context: Jesus and the Suffering World* (Minneapolis: Fortress, 2003). Hall writes that "the future of the Christian faith in the world seems quite uncertain" and that whatever survives "will have to achieve greater depths of wisdom and courage than most of what has transpired . . . throughout the fifteen-hundred-odd years of Christendom" (9–10).

4. Tom Wright, *The Day the Revolution Began: Rethinking the Meaning of Jesus' Crucifixion* (London: SPCK, 2016), 34.

how they function in much contemporary Christianity and the impression is given that these forms of faith have been superseded by the work of Christ and the gift of the Holy Spirit.

It may help us to notice some comments of Walter Brueggemann, who observes that the New Testament *does* create a new context for faith by affirming "the complete identification of God's power with God's love in the crucifixion of Jesus." In that event, "God's own life embraces the abandonment of the broken covenant." However, far from eliminating the spiritual tension found within the Hebrew Bible, the "core testimony" which is now made concerning Jesus Christ propels theology

> into issues that are as difficult for Christians as for these witnesses in the Old Testament. I would not want to conclude that the Christian faith has an easy resolution to the tension the Old Testament witnesses voice about Yahweh. I would not want to gloss over the dreadfulness of the Christian claim, both because [Good] Friday is ultimately serious, and because confessing Christians must live in the real world of Auschwitz and Hiroshima.[5]

In other words, the very nature of the messianic claim made for Jesus, that in his life, death and resurrection a *world revolution* has commenced, actually increases the level of tension experienced by believers when the evidence of human history throughout the Common Era – and especially in the modern period – provides grounds for a Christian counter-testimony.[6] In what follows I wish to explore the evidence for precisely such a lament tradition within the New Testament.

If the Hebrew Bible rests upon the core testimony of witnesses who encountered the reality of a righteous and liberating God through unusual, history-making events, the New Testament reflects a similar pattern in which eyewitnesses of the life and death of Jesus Christ share their conviction that they have experienced the turning point in human history. The author of 1 John could not make any clearer his overwhelming sense of the privilege of being a witness with the responsibility of bearing truthful testimony to the significance of the life of Jesus:

---

5. Brueggemann, *Theology of the Old Testament*, 311–312. He goes on to say: "I do not imagine Christians know a lot more or much that is different from what these candid witnesses in ancient Israel knew."

6. On the same day I typed these words it was reported that the Bulletin of Atomic Scientists had reset its symbolic Doomsday Clock to two minutes to midnight. The Bulletin's president said, "To call the world's nuclear situation dire is to understate the danger and its immediacy." *The Guardian*, 26 January 2018.

> That which was from the beginning, *which we have heard, which we have seen with our eyes, which we have looked at and our hands have touched* – this we proclaim concerning the Word of life. The life appeared; *we have seen it and testify to it*, and we proclaim to you the eternal life, which was with the Father and has appeared to us. We proclaim to you *what we have seen and heard*, so that you also may have fellowship with us. (1 John 1:1–3)

The repetition of the words "seen" and "heard" reflect an undiminished sense of wonder and amazement resulting from the living encounter with Jesus of Nazareth, while the phrase "our hands have touched" suggests a physicality and intimacy of relationship which leaves the witness at the extreme limit of what human language is capable of describing. As Richard Bauckham says, what sets the history of Jesus apart from normal experience is the conviction that this person embodied a supreme disclosure of God, leaving the eyewitnesses overcome with "wonder and thanksgiving in the presence of incomparable 'wonder-fullness.'"[7]

In the above discussion we have mentioned the Hebrew term *shalom* on a number of occasions and I want to use this word as a kind of lens with which to explore the core testimony of the Jesus movement. The word is frequently translated as "peace" but its meaning is far broader than this English term might suggest, especially if (as is often the case) "peace" is understood to mean simply the absence of war and conflict. In a wide-ranging study of the meaning of *shalom* in the Hebrew Scriptures, Brueggemann says that it encapsulates the "central vision of world history in the Bible," and that this embraces the whole created world, with "every creature in community with every other, living in harmony and security toward the joy and well-being of every other creature."[8] Certainly *shalom* anticipates the ending of armed conflict as nations "beat their swords into ploughshares" (Isa 2:4), but it envisions this as a consequence of a radical change of heart, resulting in a state of well-being which extends to the whole created world.

---

7. Richard Bauckham, *Jesus and the Eyewitnesses: The Gospels as Eyewitness Testimony* (Grand Rapids, MI: Eerdmans, 2006), 500. Bauckham demonstrates the crucial nature of eyewitness testimony as the foundation of the New Testament literature in a manner which parallels Brueggemann's recognition of its importance in relation to the Hebrew Bible. He relates this to the repeated quests for the historical Jesus and concludes, "When the quest for the historical Jesus discounts what the witnesses claim in the interests of what is readily credible by the standards of historical analogy, that is, ordinary experience, it reduces revelation to the triviality of what we knew or could know anyway" (501).

8. Walter Brueggemann, *Living toward a Vision: Biblical Reflections on Shalom* (New York: United Church Press, 1976), 15.

In creation the forces of chaos are opposed by God's powerful will for *orderly fruitfulness*. In historic community the forces of injustice and exploitation are opposed by God's will for *responsible, equitable justice*, which yields security. In personal existence, driven, anxious self-seeking is opposed by God's will for *generous caring*. The biblical vision of *shalom* functions always as a firm rejection of values and life-styles that seek security and well-being in manipulative ways at the expense of another part of creation, another part of community, or a brother or sister. The vision of the biblical way affirms that communal well-being comes by living God's dream and not by idolatrous self-aggrandizement.[9]

In the period following the destruction of Jerusalem and the exile in Babylon, this key term took on new meaning as it was related to a growing messianic hope of an age to come in which the whole world would witness a divine act of deliverance and salvation akin to a *new creation*. *Shalom* retained its connection to the hope of peace, justice and well-being, but its meaning was deepened by its relationship to the prophetic hope of a new world and a *messianic* ruler.

Many of the Jews whose parents and grandparents had been exiled in Babylon, or had fled to Egypt when the city of Jerusalem was overrun and destroyed, remained in the lands of exile, so creating a permanent Jewish diaspora which, to a greater or lesser degree, became integrated within new cultural contexts. Indeed, new prophetic voices were heard in this situation, reminding the exiles of their true identity and announcing an enlarged vision of God's *shalom* beyond the trauma and distress of the past. Isaiah 40, with its repeated assurance of divine comfort and the radiant promise of an unprecedented new beginning, is a direct response to the laments we have heard being uttered in the shattered city of Jerusalem, with their repeated complaint that "there is no-one to comfort." When the great prophet of the exile goes on to ask why Israel continues to say "My way is hidden from the LORD; my cause is disregarded by my God" (Isa 40:27) it looks as though a new generation of Jewish exiles had become locked into a spirituality and liturgy of lament and so was unable to hope for a world different from that of the empire of Babylon. Isaiah 40 and the great "Book of Comfort" which it opens is a reminder that a spirit of lament and the sense of God's *absence* may last for a very long time, but that when the work of healing is finally completed

---

9. Brueggemann, *Living toward a Vision*, 20.

a new and unimagined hope can emerge in response to a fresh vision of the universal purpose of God and his promise of *shalom*.

The communication of this new revelation of the reign of God involved a change of language as, particularly in Egypt, Hebrew and Aramaic ceased to be the mother tongues of the diaspora and were replaced by Greek. In this situation the need for a translation of the Jewish Scriptures from Hebrew to Greek became urgent, and when this was achieved in Alexandria in the shape of the Septuagint the word *shalom* was rendered as *eirene* in Greek. In this way the hope of the Jewish people, birthed with the call of Father Abraham and the promise of blessing to all nations, refined through great suffering and the seeming impossibility of its fulfilment, and dramatically enlarged and clarified by the post-exilic prophets, was to pass into the New Testament and become a fundamental aspect of the core testimony of the Jesus movement. Ulrich Mauser describes how a

> tone of joy and triumph permeates much of the New Testament, *and its frequent mention of peace is one of the reasons for it.* The remarkable frequency of the phrase "the God of peace" alone suggests that in the word "peace" some writers of the New Testament, especially the apostle Paul, found an appropriate vehicle *to concentrate the whole content of the Christian gospel.* In the gospel of Jesus Christ something unprecedented, something utterly unexpected, something of ultimate validity had appeared in the world, and one of the best ways to speak of this cheerful news was its summation in the word *eirene*.[10]

However, after the Hebrew word *shalom* had been translated into Greek it faced the challenge posed by a third language as Latin accompanied the spread and dominance of the Roman Empire with its claim to be the agent of universal peace through the celebrated Pax Romana. If the first-century Jewish followers of Jesus of Nazareth interpreted his life, teaching and death in the light of the promise of the coming of *shalom*, so that the theological term "peace" becomes a kind of shorthand which "captures the whole meaning of the Christ event," *the question of the relationship of the gospel to the claims made by the Roman Empire was (and is) unavoidable.* Klaus Wengst concludes that

> at the focal point of the New Testament, the testimony to the death and resurrection of Jesus, two completely opposed modes of peace

---

10. Ulrich Mauser, *The Gospel of Peace: A Scriptural Message for Today's World* (Louisville, KY: Westminster John Knox, 1992), 28–29; emphasis added. In the following discussion I owe much to Mauser's valuable work.

clash. There is the Pax Romana in the name of which Jesus was executed, a peace produced and secured from the then centre of power, above all by military means, an order going out from the metropolis and orientated upon it. On the other hand, there is the interruption of violence . . . there is peace and reconciliation as the abolition of oppositions and enmity, as new creation [*shalom*] which takes shape on the periphery of society.[11]

In January 2018 I drove from Glasgow in Scotland to Stratford-upon-Avon in the heart of England to see a play performed by members of the Royal Shakespeare Company over two nights. With the title *Imperium* (and adapted from Robert Harris's Cicero trilogy), the drama focused on the life of the Roman orator Cicero and his lifelong struggle to defend the Roman Republic from the dictatorship of soldiers and warlords. Catiline, Julius Caesar, Pompey, Mark Anthony and Octavian all passed before our eyes on the stage, rising and falling in the relentless power struggles at the heart of the greatest empire the world had seen. I sat next to a gentleman who expressed surprise that I had made such a long journey to be present on the two evenings and he asked me why I had done this. I explained that my major interest was in the New Testament and that, besides being attracted by a magnificent piece of theatre, I knew that what we witnessed on the stage of the Swan Theatre provided valuable insight into the context within which the documents which make up that body of literature were written. This was the world of Matthew, Mark and Luke, of Paul and of John of Patmos. Even more to the point, it was the world of Jesus of Nazareth since the Galilee which was his home and provided the geographical and cultural context of his ministry was being drastically disturbed and changed by the imperial power of the Roman colonizers. Octavian, who was last to appear on the RSC stage, rose to power under the guidance of Julius Caesar and was hailed as a son of god who had subdued his enemies and rebellious peoples, so ushering in an era of world peace – the Pax Romana. I told my conversation partner that *Imperium* clarified my understanding of the vicious power struggles at the heart of the empire while strengthening my conviction of the uniqueness of God's *shalom* ushered in by the humble carpenter from Nazareth who came to be described as "the Prince of Peace."

In the Gospel of Luke the announcement of the arrival of Christ is declared to be the source of "great joy . . . for all the people" (2:10) and this is associated with the coming of peace on earth. The contrast between this announcement

---

11. Klaus Wengst, *Pax Romana and the Peace of Jesus Christ* (London: SCM, 1987), 4.

and the Roman boast that the pacification of the nations through massive military force was the god-ordained goal of history becomes clear when Jesus's birth narrative begins with Caesar Augustus issuing a decree that a census be held throughout the empire.[12] The dominance of the imperial power, seen in the demand that people must travel at Caesar's command to facilitate a stocktaking of the subjects of his rule, and thereby the sources of taxation, stands in direct contrast to the peacemaker-child, wrapped in strips of cloth and laid in an animal feed-box. Luke surely intends irony in this picture; Caesar's decree drives "the unborn Messiah to Bethlehem that he might be born just as God 'spoke through the mouth of his holy prophets from of old'" (1:70). The readers of the gospel – including, of course, the "most excellent Theophilus," possibly a high-status person attracted to the Jesus movement later in the century – are confronted "with an image of Israel's Messiah that could not be more incongruous with the pomp and might of Emperor Augustus on his throne, commanding the world at will."[13]

The depiction of Christ as the peacemaker and the setting of this claim within the context of imperial power pervades Luke's writing so that the word "peace" comes close "to being a theological term that captures the whole meaning of the Christ event."[14] The language of the birth narrative, with its angelic announcement of peace on earth, is echoed at the other end of the gospel in the praise of the crowds welcoming Jesus on his final entry into Jerusalem. Note the close parallel between these two outbursts of praise, angelic and human:

---

12. S. R. F. Price quotes many ascriptions of praise to the Emperor Augustus, including the following statement from the assembly of the province of Asia, issued a few years before Jesus's birth: "Whereas the providence which divinely ordered our lives created with zeal and munificence the most perfect good for our lives by producing Augustus and filling him with virtue for the benefaction of mankind, sending us and those after us a saviour who put an end to war and established all things; and whereas Caesar [Augustus] when he appeared exceeded the hopes of all who had anticipated good tidings . . . not even leaving those to come any hope of surpassing him; and whereas the birthday of the god marked for the world the beginning of good tidings through his coming . . ." *Rituals and Power: The Roman Imperial Cult in Asia Minor* (Cambridge: Cambridge University Press, 1986), 54.

13. Karl Allen Kuhn, *Luke the Elite Evangelist* (Collegeville, MN: Liturgical, 2010), 94. Notice the contrast between the rejoicing in the birth narrative of Luke and the tears and bitterness which accompany the same event in Matthew. In the words of Scott Ellington, "Just as the cry of the Israelite slaves initiated God's deliverance in the Exodus, so too the initiation of his Exodus of all creation through the birth of Emmanuel finds its genesis in the tears brought about by innocent suffering, obscene corruption, and inconsolable loss." Thus, in Matthew the first word of God's salvation "is not a shout of joy, but a cry of pain." *Risking Truth: Reshaping the World through Prayers of Lament* (Eugene, OR: Pickwick, 2008), 174.

14. Mauser, *Gospel of Peace*, 46.

> Glory to God in the highest,
>> and on earth peace to men on whom his favour rests. (2:14)

> Blessed is the king who comes in the name of the Lord!
> Peace in heaven and glory in the highest! (19:38)

While these hymns of praise deploy similar language and must be intended to bookend Luke's gospel with acclamations of the peacemaker, there is a highly significant contrast between the two texts. The angelic song at the birth of Jesus includes an "insight into what is not manifest on the plane of earthly history" in that the humble birth of a helpless infant is declared to be in accordance with the glory God possesses high above the earth, "*but it is also the moment when the peace corresponding to God's glory in heaven takes hold on earth to transform this earth into a land of peace.*"[15]

By contrast, when the crowds burst into praise as Jesus is about to enter Jerusalem and its temple, they lack the angelic insight and focus their celebration on what they have seen with their own eyes as Jesus's life and teaching, his healing and deliverance of captives, made the glory and peace of heaven visible to them. Mauser reaches a conclusion which is directly relevant to our concerns in this book:

> The angels had seen, in Jesus' birth, an event that confirms God's glory in heaven and spreads God's peace on earth. But the disciples, in retrospect of Jesus' works and in entering the king's city, can ascribe glory and peace only to the realm above, "in heaven peace, and glory in the highest heaven" (Luke 19:38, lit.). *To their perception it is not yet truthful to echo the angels' choir word for word.* It is clear to them that God's glory and peace were manifest in Jesus' life among them. *But to declare "peace on earth" remains premature.* What is the reason for this incongruity, for this persistence in reservations? The answer is given by the evangelist in placing, immediately after the disciples' homage, a scene in which Jesus, looking at the city *laments* over the condition and fate of Jerusalem (Luke 19:41–44).[16]

The use of the word "lament" here is obviously significant since it reminds us that the path of Jesus was frequently marked with grief and tragedy, suggesting that for him the traditions within the Hebrew Bible which spoke

---

15. Mauser, 48; emphasis added.
16. Mauser, 48; emphasis added.

of the divine *pathos* were not only familiar but must have provided a crucial spiritual resource with which he identified completely. Jeremiah's anguish at the repudiation of his message and his person, and the deep pain arising from the knowledge of the terrible tragedy about to fall upon his city and its people, would surely have been in the mind of Jesus as he witnessed this tragic history being repeated and, with tear-stained face, cried out: "If you, even you, had only known on this day what would bring you *peace* – but now it is hidden from your eyes" (19:42).[17]

Ulrich Mauser concludes that although peace on earth had been initiated by the man whose birth the angel choirs had praised, it had not conquered the world. Salvation was *now and not yet* and the "dark shadow of this rejection of peace in Jerusalem already falls on the disciples' praise of God's glory and grace."[18] Do we not discover here at the very heart of the Christian story a dialectic between the core testimony of Jesus's followers, including the authors of the gospels, and a counter-testimony arising from resistance to God's *shalom*, often manifested by such hatred and violence as to justify the term "demonic"? The in-breaking of the kingdom of God, and with it the coming of *peace*, is the source of great joy, but as Mauser says, the gospels are "not fairy tales in which a paradise restored is offered without regard to competing and hostile realities." The Synoptic Gospels make very clear the fact that the peace of Christ is an "embattled peace" and that his followers will need patience, hope and perseverance in the face of strong and often violent opposition. *In other words, the kinds of historical circumstances which created experiences which resulted in the language and spirituality of lament in the Hebrew Bible form a crucial part of the context within which the good news of the gospel itself comes to birth.*

At this point it is important to recall that the written gospels appeared in the second half of the first century as a massive crisis deepened within Palestinian Judaism that eventually exploded in the form of the Roman-Jewish war of 66–70 CE, a conflict which reached its terrible climax in the destruction of Jerusalem amid scenes of unspeakable barbarism and human

---

17. Sean Freyne notes that Jeremiah's clash with the priestly authorities in the Jerusalem temple was "a well-remembered precedent" with respect to the ministry of Jesus. However, he also notes the contrasts between the two situations in that Jesus "lived in Roman Palestine, dominated by imperial values as these were mediated by the Herodian dynasty." Herod's spectacular building projects had transformed the temple and the city, creating an urban landscape to rival other temple-cities across the eastern empire. This context reveals that Jesus's actions posed a challenge "to the imperial power that basked in the reflected glory of this extraordinary architectural statement." *Jesus: A Jewish Galilean – A New Reading of the Jesus Story* (London: T&T Clark, 2004), 164–165.

18. Mauser, *Gospel of Peace*, 49.

suffering. In 68 CE, Vespasian, soon to become emperor, launched a military campaign intended to utterly crush Jewish rebellion once and for all and to pacify Palestine: "He marched his heavily armed legions down through Galilee towards Judaea, and . . . left a scorched-earth trail of mercilessly plundered villages – and hillsides littered with crucified insurrectionists." The Jewish historian Josephus describes scenes of horrific violence when the Roman legions finally surrounded Jerusalem, crucifying those who fled the ruins by nailing them to crosses in different postures by way of mockery, "and their number was so great that there was not enough room for the crosses and not enough crosses for the bodies."[19] The precise dating of the Synoptic Gospels remains a matter of debate, but it is certain that they appeared when this crisis filled the horizon, so that Myers suggests that Mark, for example, "wrote during the darkest days of that conflict, and it fundamentally shaped his work."[20]

The core testimony of the eyewitnesses of the life, death and resurrection of Jesus of Nazareth is that his appearance on earth represents the turning point in history and brings to fulfilment the promise of Yahweh's *shalom* and, with it, the reign of God in justice and righteousness. The *words* of Jesus represent the culminating point of the long tradition of Hebrew prophecy, articulating "God's dream" of a renewal and transformation on earth so extensive as to embrace the whole of creation and both individual and social life. The *deeds* of Jesus vindicated his radical message while also prefiguring the new world, acting as visible, concrete signs of the new age in which peace, justice and love would reshape the human family and eliminate enmity and conflict between peoples. Ulrich Mauser comments that, in combination with the proclamation of the arrival of the kingdom of God, the narratives of healing and deliverance "are flares in the night announcing the coming of a day whose light will enlighten the earth at large, down to its last crevice and corner." In

---

19. Quoted in Martin Hengel, *Crucifixion in the Ancient World and the Folly of the Message of the Cross* (Philadelphia: Fortress, 1977), 26.

20. Ched Myers, "Mark 13 in a Different Imperial Context," in *Mark: Gospel of Action – Personal and Community Responses*, ed. John Vincent (London: SPCK, 2006), 168–169. Warren Carter's commentary on Matthew locates that gospel after the destruction of Jerusalem in "a context of conflict" in which the community of Jesus's followers "feels persecuted" and "struggles to make sense of the pain and hostility." *Matthew and the Margins: A Socio-Political and Religious Reading* (London: T&T Clark, 2000), 33. With regard to Luke's writing, see C. Kavin Rowe, *World Upside Down: Reading Luke–Acts in the Graeco-Roman Age* (Oxford: Oxford University Press, 2009). Richard Bauckham has noted "many and unmistakable allusions to (and even quotations from) the psalms of lament" in the passion narratives of all four gospels. He comments that in these texts, "Jesus in his passion is identified with all who had prayed or could pray these psalms for themselves, all who suffer the meaningless abandonment from which they cry to God." *The Bible in the Contemporary World: Exploring Texts and Contexts – Then and Now* (London: SPCK, 2016), 130–131.

particular, the feeding narratives demonstrate God's concern for the most basic needs of human beings and their protection from rapacious economic systems which threaten their very survival. The epiphany of the true king ushers in a new world in which the redemptive powers of heaven are unleashed "so that a desolate and arid land becomes the scene of a meal for multitudes who are preserved from hunger."[21]

This combination of word and deed, of a prophetic proclamation of unprecedented courage and clarity accompanied by a life of overflowing mercy and compassion, brought hope and liberation to the oppressed and marginalized, while triggering reactions from both sides of a deeply divided society. On the one hand, the political and religious authorities who were the beneficiaries of the dominant system identified Jesus as the latest and most serious threat to their power and privilege, as the terrible words with which the priestly class respond to Pilate make clear, demanding the crucifixion of Jesus even as they pledge their loyalty to Caesar (John 19:15–16). On the other hand, members of Jewish radical movements advocating anti-imperial violence were offended by the refusal of Jesus to endorse their ethnic nationalism and the call to armed resistance.[22] Consequently, the *words* and *deeds* of Jesus provoked the crisis which led him to *the death of the cross*, which was itself to become a fundamental aspect of the core testimony of his followers.

The Day God Died . . .

We have already noticed both the widespread use of crucifixion as a deterrent to acts of resistance and rebellion against Roman power, and the extreme cruelty which this form of punishment involved. Since it took place in public spaces it involved the total humiliation of victims and their complete dehumanization. It was reserved for dangerous criminals, political radicals and the poorest of people, including rebellious slaves whose actions were deemed to pose a threat to the dominant order. Martin Hengel points out that a large segment of the population throughout the empire accepted the ideology of the Pax Romana and so welcomed the peace and security which was claimed to flow from it,

---

21. Mauser, *Gospel of Peace*, 57–60.

22. Sean Freyne comments: "The fact that Jesus' lifestyle was accompanied by a call for total trust in Yahweh, the creator God, as this was expressed in the Jubilee and Sabbath year legislation, no matter how utopian such a call might have appeared, indicates just how incensed he was by the situation that he encountered. It was these conditions, so alien to the Biblical ideals of a restored Israel, that acted as the catalyst for his apocalyptic imagination to challenge the existing unjust structures, not by the traditional means of a militant resistance, but by a new and creative interpretation of the kingdom of God." *Jewish Galilean*, 140.

with the result that crucified victims were "defamed both socially and ethically in popular awareness." The idea that God might be associated with such a victim, crucified as a threat to Roman law and justice, provoked derision and the suspicion of insanity. In Hengel's words, identifying God with death "in the form of a crucified Jewish manual worker from Galilee in order to break the power of death" and bring salvation to humankind could only seem folly and madness to people of ancient times. And he adds, tellingly, "Even now, any genuine theology will have to be measured against the test of this scandal."[23]

The true horror of the death of Jesus, especially for those who had invested such huge messianic hopes in him, can only be dimly imagined. Indeed, for Christians two thousand years later the difficulty of this imaginative task is compounded by the knowledge of Easter Sunday, and then by a plethora of theological and liturgical developments which have embellished the meaning of the cross, often transmuting it into a symbol of triumph and glory. In addition, our neglect of the tradition of lament in the Bible further hinders our grasp of the significance of Jesus's shameful death and makes us reluctant to linger too long with his followers at the cross, including women "who mourned and wailed for him" (Luke 23:27). Lament, the outpouring of a grief to God concerning an event which lay beyond all comprehension, signalling nothing less than the death of God's messiah and the termination of hope, is here discovered to be at the very core of the gospel narrative, both in the trauma of Jesus's devoted and loving followers and on his own lips in the cry of dereliction borrowed from the psalms of lament which he knew so well.

Of course, after the resurrection the *meaning* of the crucifixion of Jesus was understood in a new light and the centuries-long attempt to interpret the death of the cross commenced. That task is both valid and important, but the danger remains that we move too quickly from the cross to the empty tomb with the result that theology becomes associated with abstract theories of atonement which are invariably divorced from the harsh reality of the historical death of Jesus on the hill of Calvary.[24] Theological theory can too easily

---

23. Hengel, *Crucifixion*, 88–89. Notice also Tom Holland's statement: "No death was more excruciating, more contemptible, than crucifixion. To be hung naked, 'long in agony, swelling with ugly weals on shoulders and chest,' helpless to beat away the clamorous birds: such a fate, Roman intellectuals agreed, was the worst imaginable." He quotes the historian Tacitus as justifying such a form of execution as the only way to control the vast army of slaves who came from every corner of the world, "practicing strange customs, and foreign cults, or none – and it is only by means of terror that we can hope to coerce such scum." *Dominion: The Making of the Western Mind* (London: Little Brown, 2019), xiv. Hengel, *Crucifixion*, 88–89.

24. In a very significant study to which we will give more attention below, Alan Lewis writes that the "impossible foolishness" of the cross, the story which "unites God with a human corpse," is "the supreme test of our willingness not to conform the story to what we already understand,

become a distorting mirror which conceals the true depths of the suffering and humiliation of Good Friday *and obscures, even to the point of completely forgetting, the first and primary lesson this teaches us concerning the being of God.* In the words of Martin Hengel,

> the earliest Christian message of the crucified messiah demonstrated the "solidarity" of the love of God with the unspeakable suffering of those who were tortured and put to death by human cruelty. . . . This suffering has continued down to the present century in a "passion story" which we cannot even begin to assess, a "passion story" which is based on human sin in which we all without exception participate, as beings who live under the power of death. In the person and the fate of this one man Jesus of Nazareth this saving "solidarity" of God with us is given its historical and physical form.[25]

. . . And the Day After!

A number of times in this discussion I have used the phrase "cross and resurrection" as a way of referring to the Easter story. This is, of course, a very common way of speaking and signifies that the crucifixion of Jesus and the empty tomb, the horror of Good Friday and the surprise of Easter Sunday, *together* constitute the revolution to which we have referred earlier. Yet in using language in this way the time span of the narrative in the gospels is collapsed and so bypasses the reality of the intervening Sabbath, that long Saturday which occurred between these two events and must therefore be considered as an integral part of the Easter story. What shall we say about that day, the day *after* the crucifixion, when the corpse of Jesus lay still and lifeless in the tomb and the process of decomposition had already commenced? We are surely faced with a situation in which the followers of Jesus are rendered

---

but to reconform our understanding to the story that we hear." He warns of the danger that in trying to conceive and understand this singular event we "suppress the very revolution that the story embodies, naturalize the alienness of its ideas, tame the violence it does to our logic, and anesthetize its wounding of our pride." *Between Cross and Resurrection: A Theology of Holy Saturday* (Grand Rapids, MI: Eerdmans, 2001), 26–27.

25. Hengel, *Crucifixion*, 88. Note the comment of Claus Westermann: "If the gospel story of the passion is presented in the words of Psalm 22, the authors quite obviously wanted to say that Christ had taken up the lament of those people who suffer, that he too had entered into suffering. Hence, his suffering is a part of the history of those who have suffered, who have found their language in the Psalms of lament. With his suffering and dying, therefore, Jesus could not have had only the sinner in mind; he must also have been thinking of those who suffer." *Praise and Lament*, 275.

numb and speechless, existing in a kind of limbo familiar to all who have lost a loved friend in tragic circumstances, but here magnified a thousand times by the hopes invested in this person and by the disgraceful and dishonourable nature of his end. In fact, so terrible does the experience of this day seem, so completely devoid of meaning, that we do not care to dwell upon it and have a tendency to pass over it as a mere incident without much significance in relation to the story as a whole.

This is, as Alan Lewis has so convincingly shown, a great mistake because Easter Saturday "is not an in-between day which simply waits for the morrow, but is an empty void, a nothing, shapeless, meaningless, and anticlimactic: simply the day after the end."[26] He observes that these long, empty hours, filled with memories and regret, contained no suggestion that triumph and vindication lay just around the corner. Indeed, the overwhelming sense of a terrible ending extends into Easter Sunday itself since the disciples whom Luke reports as walking away from Jerusalem on the road to Emmaus have downcast faces and betray in their mood and language that their hopes have been brought to a shattering end, leaving them face to face with an abyss of meaninglessness and despair (Luke 24:13–24).[27] That long, desolate Sabbath which bisects death and resurrection may not be ignored as though it were merely a kind of hyphen between the words which really matter, because that day itself bears huge theological significance, reporting as it does the experience of the death of God, with all its consequences for humanity, an experience which has become the "new normal" for millions of human beings in a postmodern, globalized world. As Lewis says, we have not listened to the narrative of the gospel "until we have construed this cold, dark Sabbath as the day of atheism."[28] On that day the sounds to be heard were the boasts "from the world's satanic despots, and the strangulated wails of disbelief from their indignant, disillusioned victims."[29]

> *What we hear from Job in the Old Testament is silently uttered again in the New, on Good Friday and its sequel.* It is the outraged exclamation that God is dead. . . . In the death cry of Jesus of Nazareth there resonates the ageless, universal protest of human suffering, affronted by the crookedness of human life, whereby

---

26. Lewis, *Between Cross and Resurrection*, 31.

27. I have reflected on this narrative at length in *Moving toward Emmaus: Hope in a Time of Uncertainty* (London: SPCK, 2007).

28. Lewis, *Between Cross and Resurrection*, 56.

29. Lewis, 56.

the innocent are tortured and the diabolic flourish. Is the cry of the Crucified, "Why?" not echoed by every victim of oppression, accident, and disease, as they plead for meaning in the midst of the world's absurdity? And the silence that greets his question is the same sorrowing stillness of the cancer ward and the concentration camp.... *And those who would hear what the narrative of Christ crucified and buried really says today need simply to listen to the alienated disbelief of their own bewildered generation and to the guilty pleadings of their own lonely, disappointed hearts.*[30]

On the borders of France, Germany and Switzerland it is possible to discover three paintings which provide unforgettable visual images of the three days of the Easter story. In the lovely French town of Colmar the Musée d'Unterlinden displays an altarpiece painted in the early sixteenth century by an artist known to us as Matthias Grünewald. The side panels of this astonishing work, the Isenheim Altarpiece, stand open to display the central, shocking portrayal of the crucified Christ, his emaciated body contorted by suffering and his skin bearing the marks of some terrible disease. The picture has been described as the most unforgettable image in the whole history of Western art, in part because it abandons sanitized representations of crucifixion and confronts us with that reality in all its horror. The painting has a very particular context; it was intended for the chapel of a monastery at Isenheim, near Colmar, where monks had dedicated themselves to caring for the dying victims of a sickness called St Anthony's Fire, now believed to have been caused by eating bread infected with a parasitic fungus. The condition sapped people's strength and resulted in a skin disease which covered the victims' flesh with ugly lesions and sores, the very same marks which disfigure the body of Christ as he hangs upon the cross. Grünewald, who was himself to die in poverty but whose meagre possessions at the time of his passing included twenty-seven of Martin Luther's sermons, understood the Easter message and offered the sick and despairing the assurance that the Christ "from whom men [hid] their faces" had indeed taken up "our infirmities and carried our sorrows" (Isa 53:3–4).

Not too far away, across the border with Switzerland, the city of Basel was the home of another great artist influenced by the Reformation, Hans Holbein. He was familiar with the Isenheim Altarpiece and was to take a similar approach to Grünewald in his own extraordinary depiction of the Easter Sabbath Day in his painting *The Dead Christ*. In some ways this image is even more shocking than the one in Colmar in that, while there were many

---

30. Lewis, 56; emphasis added.

artistic precedents for painting the crucifixion, few artists had dared to take the dead body of Jesus as a subject, and certainly no one presented it with such shocking realism. Much later Fyodor Dostoyevsky sought out this picture and stood transfixed before it for a very long time, his wife saying that he seemed to be about to have an epileptic fit as a result of contemplating this image. In his novel *The Idiot* the great Russian author made frequent references to this painting and had one character say, "Why, some people may lose their faith by looking at that picture."[31]

However, Holbein had been profoundly influenced by the Reformation and his intention was to present the stark reality of Holy Saturday as the day when God really did embrace death, so that in his astonishing painting the real meaning of the incarnation was laid bare, stripped of all evasion and sentimentality. "The Bible spoke of the Word of God becoming flesh. That flesh suffered death. In the black secrecy of the tomb that flesh began to decay. Grasp this, Holbein says, and you begin to understand what Incarnation is about. Grasp this and the miracle of Resurrection will strike you with full force."[32]

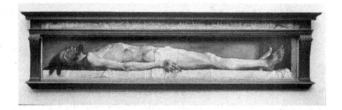

Figure 3.1: *The Body of the Dead Christ in the Tomb.* **Hans Holbein the Younger, 1521. Photo courtesy of © Kunstmusem, Basel/Bridgeman Art Library.**

For the third picture we must retrace our steps to Colmar and walk round the Isenheim Altarpiece to view the central panel on the reverse side which, after the horror of Messiah's death, literally took this viewer's breath away. Here is Easter Sunday as it has never been seen before: Christ not simply raised from death, but his body transformed, the skin which had been so disfigured by the disease ravaging central Europe now glowing with a purity and beauty which befits what Paul described as "the heavenly body" which is "raised in glory" (1 Cor 15:40–44).

---

31. Fyodor Dostoevsky, *The Idiot* (Harmondsworth: Penguin, 1955), 251.

32. Derek Wilson, *Hans Holbein: Portrait of an Unknown Man* (London: Phoenix, 1996), 95.

This victory of faith and hope was not, however, easily won. Having witnessed the dying agonies of so many victims of the plagues which devastated Europe, Grünewald knew very well the struggle between faith and doubt. One of the side panels of the Altarpiece depicts the temptation of St Anthony, and in the bottom right corner is a tiny piece of paper on which the artist has written the words, "Where were you good Jesus, where were you? Why did you not help me and heal my wounds?"

In a world afflicted by disease, social chaos and violence, the lament continued to be a crucial spiritual resource, and faith and hope emerged from within the dialectic discussed previously. Without that tension between faith and doubt religion becomes a form of false consciousness which refuses to confront the reality of life in a broken world and as a result is easily dismissed as empty rhetoric devoid of integrity by those who know from experience that life in this world is otherwise.

Faith During a Long Saturday

We will return to the theological and pastoral significance of the Easter story later in this book, but here I want to underline the importance of this theme and its relevance in the context of modern culture. If Alan Lewis is correct in saying that we have not properly understood the significance of the "cold, dark Sabbath" of the Easter story until we recognize it as "the day of atheism," the day when God died and was buried, does that not suggest the existence of *a vital point of contact between the gospel and a culture built on the foundation of atheism?* The European Enlightenment began a process which resulted in serious questions arising for Christian theology, in particular for inherited forms of theism. The intellectuals at the heart of this movement understood that their project involved the dismantling of an entire structure of beliefs which had until then been regarded as axiomatic. Friedrich Nietzsche's brilliant parable of the madman who ran into a market square crying out, "I am looking for God!" expressed in powerful language the implications of this movement of revolutionary change.

> How were we able to drink up the sea? Who gave us the sponge to wipe away the entire horizon? What did we do when we unchained this earth from its sun? Whither is it moving now? Whither are we moving now? Away from all suns? Are we not perpetually falling? Backward, sideward, forward, in all directions? Is there any up or down left? Are we not straying as through an infinite nothing? Do we not feel the breath of empty space? Has it not become colder?

Is more and more night not coming on all the time? Do we not hear anything yet of the noise of the gravediggers who are burying God? Do we not smell anything yet of God's decomposition? – gods, too, decompose. God is dead. God remains dead. And we have killed him. How shall we, the murderers of all murderers, console ourselves?[33]

Nietzsche describes how people standing in the square "who did not believe in God" mocked and ridiculed the madman, yet his sense of the enormity of the changes taking place, of the loss of transcendence and the unimaginable burden of responsibility about to fall on human shoulders, accurately reflected the reality of a culture in which mortal beings now aspired to replace the Creator and take full control of nature and history.

Yet again, our earlier reflections on Job come to mind; the madman in the parable glimpses the enormity of the tasks which will confront humankind in a godless future. Precisely this knowledge had caused Job to cover his mouth with his hands and confess that he had spoken of things "too wonderful for me." With the Enlightenment nothing remained "too wonderful" and modern people, armed with science and technology, would no longer acknowledge any limits to their powers. The cosmos had been (in Max Weber's famous term) "disenchanted," its mysteries opened up to human probing, discovery and manipulation, so that God was forced to retreat to the margins of the universe where his irrelevance to the emerging culture would result in his "death."

Nietzsche's parable, which may appear profoundly shocking when first encountered, suggests that, in sharp contrast to the shallow atheists who poured scorn on the madman's anguish at the loss of God, he understood the cataclysmic nature of the shift taking place within European Christendom.[34] Elsewhere Nietzsche describes the death of God as the "greatest event of modern times," explaining that the phrase signifies the historical and cultural reality that "*belief in the Christian God has become unbelievable.*" Unlike many of his contemporaries, Nietzsche recognized that the disturbances shaking the existing world were only the first tremors of a coming earthquake which would bring about the collapse of an entire way of life built over centuries on Christian foundations. For those people capable of recognizing the full extent of this event "it seems as though some sun has just gone down, some ancient profound trust

---

33. R. J. Hollingdale, ed., *A Nietzsche Reader* (Harmondsworth: Penguin, 1977), 202–203.

34. Note the comment of Terry Eagleton that Nietzsche "has a strong claim to being the first real atheist." It is he who "above all confronts the terrifying, exhilarating consequences of the death of God." *Culture and the Death of God* (New Haven: Yale University Press, 2015), 151.

had been turned round into doubt," and the coming collapse of a centuries-old culture will take with it *"our entire European morality."* He piles up words like "demolition," "destruction," "decline" and "overturning" to describe an "eclipse of the sun such as there has probably never yet been on earth."[35]

Nietzsche must have known that the gospels reported that at the moment when the crucified Jesus breathed his final breath, "darkness came over the whole land . . . , for the sun stopped shining" (Luke 23:44–45). What is more, that eclipse of the source of light and life on earth resulted in a world without horizons in which the followers of Jesus experienced the sense of abandonment and complete dislocation of the madman in the parable. Did they not feel that they were "straying through an infinite nothing" and that the world after Golgotha had become colder and darker? Had they not witnessed the death of God and found themselves confronting a future with burdens which appeared to be too heavy to bear? The disciples walking away from Jerusalem on the road to Emmaus, traumatized by the shameful crucifixion of the prophet they "had hoped . . . was going to redeem Israel," surely knew the dreadful reality of a darkened world in which God's dream of *shalom* had turned to dust and ashes. This was now a scene in which the seemingly invincible power of the rulers of this world had crushed and rubbished messianic hope, so that, in the words of yet another secular prophet in the twentieth century, the sky had become empty and the earth was "delivered into the hands of power without principles."[36]

What this means, I suggest, is that Christians who know the end of the Easter story and so confess with joy and thanksgiving that Christ is risen, must bear this testimony within a historical context which we may describe as an Easter Saturday culture. Millions of human beings are born into a one-

---

35. Hollingdale, *Nietzsche Reader*, 208–209; emphasis added. See Peter Frick, "Nietzsche: The Archetype of Pauline Deconstruction," in *Paul in the Grip of the Philosophers: The Apostle and Contemporary Continental Philosophers*, ed. Peter Frick (Minneapolis: Fortress, 2013), 15–37. Frick concludes that Nietzsche's critique of Christianity was deeply influenced by "personal observation and experience of those around him – mother, aunts, and those like them," and that his upbringing "presented him with a warped and distorted conception of the Christian faith." See also Stephen Williams, *The Shadow of the Antichrist: Nietzsche's Critique of Christianity* (Grand Rapids, MI: Baker Academic, 2006).

36. The phrase comes from Albert Camus, *The Rebel* (Harmondsworth: Penguin, 1971), 117. Camus is, of course, describing the *modern* world in what is a most profound analysis of the culture anticipated by Nietzsche, viewed from the perspective of the second half of the twentieth century. Camus writes, "How to live without grace – that is the question that dominates the nineteenth century. 'By justice,' answered all those who did not want to accept absolute nihilism. To the people who despaired of the Kingdom of Heaven, they promised the kingdom of men. . . . The question of the twentieth century . . . has gradually been specified: how to live without grace and without justice?" (192–193).

dimensional world, live their lives without access to publicly recognized experiences of transcendence, and face death as an absolute ending which drains away the meaning of existence. George Steiner, in a remarkable book entitled *Real Presences*, concluded that "where God's presence is no longer a tenable supposition and where his absence is no longer a felt, indeed overwhelming weight, certain dimensions of thought and creativity are no longer attainable."[37] The tragedy of modern Western culture is that it compels people to traverse "the long day's journey of Saturday," where the foundations are shaken, the sky darkens, the poets fall silent, language moves toward incoherence and the music dies.

This, then, is the world within which Christians share their testimony that God "wrested from the grave self-vindicating victory, authentication for the Son, and life and hope for a despairing world."[38] Yet that broken world is not some strange territory into which the messengers of hope make occasional forays before retreating to the security of a walled-off ghetto; *it is their world too, and they share in its pain and loss, its deep hunger for answers to the age-old questions which arise from its suffering, and the nagging fear arising from the threat to its very survival in the age of the Anthropocene.* Thus, the core testimony of the gospel, that the crucified one has been raised and the power of death and corruption overcome, must be shared, not with a triumphalist spirit, but with humility, compassion and a transparent honesty concerning faith's own struggles with the tragedies that persist in an Easter Saturday culture. In the words of Alan Lewis:

> The protest of unbelief is that the world is godless and unjust, a place of lovelessness, iniquity, and pain. Faith, by contrast, hears and speaks a word of promise – that nothing, however evil, can separate us from God's love, so that the world's sure destiny is peace and joy. Yet that confidence itself contains the temptation so to proclaim the world's salvation as to take no longer seriously its distancing from God through suffering, sin, and death. There is a "faith" which has forgotten what it is to doubt; a way of hearing which no longer listens to the silence; a certainty that God is close which dares not look into eyes still haunted by divine remoteness; a hope of some glory other than a crown of thorns.[39]

---

37. George Steiner, *Real Presences: Is There Anything in What We Say?* (London: Faber & Faber, 1991), 230–232.

38. Lewis, *Between Cross and Resurrection*, 97.

39. Lewis, 98.

For Reflection

> As Jesus was leaving the temple, one of his disciples said to him, "Look, Teacher! What massive stones! What magnificent buildings!"
>
> "Do you see all these great buildings?" replied Jesus. "Not one stone will be left on another; every one will be thrown down."
>
> As Jesus was sitting on the Mount of Olives opposite the temple, Peter, James, John and Andrew asked him privately, "Tell us, when will these things happen? And what will be the sign that they are all about to be fulfilled?"
>
> Jesus said to them: "Watch out that no-one deceives you. Many will come in my name, claiming, 'I am he,' and will deceive many. When you hear of wars and rumours of wars, do not be alarmed. Such things must happen, but the end is still to come. Nation will rise against nation, and kingdom against kingdom. There will be earthquakes in various places, and famines. These are the beginning of birth-pains.
>
> "You must be on your guard. You will be handed over to the local councils and flogged in the synagogues. On account of me you will stand before governors and kings as witnesses to them. And the gospel must first be preached to all nations. Whenever you are arrested and brought to trial, do not worry beforehand about what to say. Just say whatever is given you at the time, for it is not you speaking, but the Holy Spirit.
>
> "Brother will betray brother to death, and a father his child. Children will rebel against their parents and have them put to death. All men will hate you because of me, but he who stands firm to the end will be saved." (Mark 13:1–13)

Mark's Jesus insists that war, though inevitable in the world system, is emphatically not a sign of apocalyptic world transformation, despite its cataclysmic trappings. He parodies the claims of those who would market the conflict as an historic struggle. . . . War should never come as a surprise to Christians – we have been forewarned (13:23). But Jesus does not fail to remind disciples that resisting the demands of war leaders will result in systematic persecution (13:9–13). He does however, guarantee that the Holy Spirit will be our companion when we are summoned before the authorities (13:11).

Jesus' closing statement is directed to the church in every age – especially to sophisticated moderns who would dismiss this sermon as the apocalyptic ranting of primitive Christians: "What I say to you I say to all: Stay Awake!" (13:37)[40]

---

40. Ched Myers, "Mark 13," 172–174.

4

The Witness of Paul: Ecstasy and Agony

I began this book with a reference to my return from cross-cultural ministry in the rainforests of Eastern Nigeria. That hugely influential period in my own pilgrimage had begun in 1977 when my wife Joyce and I with our two small boys set sail from Tilbury Docks in London for an unknown destination somewhere in the Niger Delta. The journey on board a Nigerian cargo ship named *Ahmadu Bello* took almost five weeks, including stops at various ports around the bulge of West Africa. One morning we woke to discover that we were sailing between oil flares emitted from the drilling platforms which dotted the seas in the Gulf of Guinea, meaning that this long and eventful voyage was nearing its completion. The ship moved slowly toward one of the many streams in the delta of the great Niger River and sailed upstream to a tiny port called Koko. When we finally reached our destination we discovered that the single berth beside the river was already occupied, necessitating a delay, moored midstream until it became possible to access the dock.

Unfortunately, a colleague had driven a van some two hundred miles to meet us and transport us to the distant Cross River State where we were to make our home. This resulted in Joyce and the children disembarking and making the journey by road, while I remained on board the ship until our boxes could be offloaded. When, after considerable delay, this happened I discovered that a senior member of the ship's crew was hiring a truck to take wood which he had purchased during our stop in Takoradi, Ghana, to an area close to my destination and he kindly offered to give me a lift together with our luggage. When the truck, known in Nigeria as a Mammy Wagon, arrived, I noticed that like all such vehicles it had been given a name: *Happy Survival.* At the time I had no idea just how appropriate that title would prove to be!

After the wagon was loaded we lingered during an afternoon, then went to visit the driver's family, before finally pulling away as darkness was falling, and I realized that this was to be an overnight journey. I immediately became aware of the cacophony of sounds emerging from the surrounding bush, my first experience of the chorus of an African night with which I was to become so familiar. Eastern Nigeria was still reeling in the aftermath of the terrible Civil War which between 1967 and 1970 had devastated this part of the country, leaving the road system destroyed and in some places almost impassable. I sat up front between the driver and the sailor and listened, largely in ignorance, to their animated conversation in Pidgin English. At one point, my ears beginning to adapt to this fascinating dialect, I realized that they were discussing our chances of getting through the night without encountering armed robbers. Clearly, this was bandit country and with the road pitted with huge potholes, some large enough to almost swallow up our wagon, this was a journey involving more risk and danger than I had previously known.

I began to wonder about Joyce and the boys; did they reach the end of their journey safely? How would those precious little ones cope with our separation in these circumstances, and with such a journey? Once the imagination sets off down this kind of path there is no telling where it might end: would I actually see them again? After midnight, as the conversation between my companions faltered, I suddenly found the words with which Paul described his experiences of travel in the ancient world of the Roman Empire coming to mind with tremendous force: "I have . . . been exposed to death again and again . . . three times I was shipwrecked, I spent a night and a day in the open sea, I have been constantly on the move. I have been in danger from rivers, *in danger from bandits* . . . in danger in the city . . . in danger at sea . . . " (2 Cor 11:23–29).

That long night journey suddenly appeared in my mind in a different perspective. Not only did my situation seem somewhat tame beside the apostle's catalogue of his encounters with danger, but I recalled that he actually celebrated these experiences as opportunities to discover the grace and mercy of God. The lumbering Mercedes Benz truck *Happy Survival* began to look like a gift, an unasked-for opportunity to gain a new understanding of the context of the New Testament and the life of the apostle Paul, and perhaps to prove his claim that human weakness and vulnerability bring opportunities to prove the reality of faith and discover the divine strength.

It is biographical snippets like the one just quoted which make Paul of particular interest in relation to the subject of this book. The nature of his correspondence, as letters to real people in specific places and situations, means that we are given some access to his life in a way that has a parallel with our knowledge of the prophet Jeremiah. In addition, we have the narrative provided by Luke in the book of Acts, so that we can trace the main outline of Paul's journey from the life-changing event on the road to Damascus, to his final imprisonment in Rome, awaiting the verdict which would eventually lead to his execution.

Our concern is with the specific question: can the dialectic between faith and doubt which we have traced through the Bible to this point be found in Paul's experience? Or is this now the juncture at which faith becomes so certain and secure that it parts company with the Jewish tradition of the prayer of lament? Paul's life and work have been imagined in various ways, one of which may be described as the "heroic" Paul, triumphant over all obstacles and setbacks, planting little cells of new followers of Jesus across the eastern empire, and apparently always able to recognize and rejoice in the purpose of God no matter how great the obstacles which had to be surmounted. Does he not claim to have learned to "be content *whatever* the circumstances" (Phil 4:11)? And at the climax of the story, as Luke tells it, despite the seeming failure to complete his declared aims in mission, triumph still overcomes tragedy as he is granted a "rented house" where he "welcomed all who came to see him" and boldly "and without hindrance . . . preached the kingdom of God and taught about the Lord Jesus Christ" (Acts 28:30–31). Imprisonment in the imperial capital appears to be included in the "all things" which, Paul had told the followers of Jesus in Rome years earlier, work together for good within the divine purpose (Rom 8:28).

There is, however, another side to this optimistic picture. We noticed in the previous chapter how the very nature of the messianic claims made for Jesus necessarily increased the pressures on faith when historical developments provided little concrete evidence that the turning point of all the ages had arrived. Indeed, the New Testament literature itself contains clear and repeated evidence of this tension as Jewish nationalism became ever more militant and Rome tightened its grip on power and asserted its universal dominance in the form of strident propaganda and violent, repressive military actions. Little wonder then that the New Testament contains reports of "scoffers" who dismissed the Christian claims of a revolutionary transformation and asked, "Where is this 'coming' he promised?" (2 Peter 3:4).

Paul's development of the messianic tradition involved taking the message which had originated in a Palestinian setting with Jesus and his disciples and proclaiming it as the hope of peace for the whole world – the Pax Christi. The Jewish Messiah was also the Gentile Lord, so that the announcement of God's *shalom*, of a new era of redemption and reconciliation for all nations, had a universal reach. Nowhere is this clearer, perhaps, than in the words with which the letter to the Romans closes, where Paul speaks of "my gospel" as based upon a revelation of "the mystery hidden for long ages past" but now unveiled "so that all nations might believe and obey him" (Rom 16:25–27). Thus, Paul's gospel, which he understands to be both international and even cosmic in its significance, must be made known to the very ends of the earth (which of course demands the process of cultural and linguistic translation). We are clearly dealing with an announcement of epochal significance since it involves a vision and hope for the transformation of the world and all its peoples. It is precisely the greatness and glory of these claims which raises the stakes for those who embrace them and base their entire lives upon them, since when history tells a different story, as it seemed to do in the tragedies of the second half of the first century, such claims go against the grain of actual lived experience, *making the need for a Christian prayer of lament as real and spiritually urgent as ever.*

Paul's language describing the abuse and humiliation he endured as the messenger of the cross suggests that the image of the "heroic Paul" is misleading if it results in ignoring his humanity, pain and suffering.[1] As with letters which modern missionaries send to their supporters, we must sometimes read between the lines to discern the realities of disappointments, struggles and frustration with people and with God which may be concealed beneath the surface of positive reports of success and advance. There are many points in Paul's letters where it is possible to "read between the lines" and detect the enormous pressures which weighed upon him and posed questions for the messianic faith which he proclaimed across the empire. In his correspondence such questions remain largely private concerns, subordinated to his calling to nurture the faith of his converts and to support them in the very real pressures they faced as people of low status, lacking honour within Roman, urban culture.

In the remainder of this chapter I want to examine a few examples of statements which clearly suggest the depths of Paul's personal struggles and lead to the conclusion that his confidence in the power of the gospel to bring healing, reconciliation and a world transformed by grace did not go unchallenged and required a dynamic hope in the face of evidence which appeared to justify claims that it was the Roman Empire which had ushered in "the end of history."

---

1. See the remarkable series of texts in 2 Corinthians in which the apostle's anguish and struggle are described: 1:3–11; 4:7–12; 6:3–10; 12:7–10.

The Scum of the Earth

As we noticed in the previous chapter, Paul's mission took place in the context of the spread of Roman imperialism with its ideology of peace through conquest and the coming of a golden age for the world. During the reign of Augustus the concept of world empire was developed in new ways in which a sharper than ever distinction was made between the Roman "self" and the barbarian "other," the two "never allowed to occupy the same visual space except in opposition to one another."[2] In a series of studies Davina Lopez has shown the importance of *visual* representations of the relationship between ruler and ruled in the form of sculptures, monuments, inscriptions in public spaces, and on coins.[3] Conquered peoples throughout the vast area ruled by Rome were in this way constantly reminded of their place in the order which was now imposed upon the world and of the consequences of questioning that order, let alone attempting to rebel against it. As Lopez says,

> Such images of "peace" accomplished through victory over the enemy served both to represent and naturalize Roman world power, creating an adaptable notion of what counts as "normal" within this ideology. Augustus and the Julio-Claudians imagined themselves uniquely fit to rule a world of nations whose two poles, the ruler and the ruled, defined the whole cosmos in gendered and racialized terms.[4]

One of the most famous of these visual images, and perhaps the most profoundly moving of them all, is the marble sculpture *The Dying Gaul*, which shows a defeated tribal warrior at the point of death. However noble this figure may seem, the fact is that the depiction of his fate was intended as a sober warning to barbarians, be they Gauls, Galatians, Celts, Spaniards – or, for that matter, Jews – that this would be the inevitable and certain result of a refusal

---

2. Davina Lopez, "Visualizing Significant Otherness: Reimagining Paul(ine) Studies) through Hybrid Lenses," in *The Colonized Apostle: Paul through Postcolonial Eyes*, ed. Christopher Stanley (Minneapolis: Fortress, 2011), 80.

3. See Davina Lopez, *Apostle to the Conquered: Reimagining Paul's Mission* (Minneapolis: Fortress Press, 2008); "Visualizing Significant Otherness," 74–94; and "Visual Perspectives: Imag(in)ing the Big Pauline Picture" in *Studying Paul's Letters: Contemporary Perspectives and Methods*, ed. Joseph Marchal (Minneapolis: Fortress Press, 2012): 93–116. On imagery on Roman coins, see Larry Kreitzer, *Striking New Images: Roman Imperial Coinage and the New Testament World* (Sheffield: Sheffield Academic Press, 1996). He discusses, among many other examples, the striking of new coins by Vespasian and Titus following the destruction of Jerusalem in 70 CE. One of these depicts "a dejected female impersonation" of Judea "sitting beside a palm tree, often with her arms bound behind her," while the obverse shows the victorious Caesar.

4. Lopez, "Visualizing Significant Otherness," 80–81.

to submit to the predestined order of the world. As Brigitte Kahl puts it, for the Romans, "conquering the world was not an act of imperial expansion but rather a meritorious deed on behalf of civilized humanity," and she concludes that the bent back of the Dying Gaul became "a stepping stone to world power."[5]

Figure 4.1: *The Dying Gaul.* **Roman marble copy of Hellenistic original. Musei Capitolini, Rome. Photo "Sculpture of the Dying Gaul" by Bebo86 / CCBY-SA 3.0.**

At this point we are compelled to ask: how does the image of *The Dying Gaul* relate to that of *The Dead Christ*? Readers might want to pause here and reflect on the two images, as it were, side by side. As we saw in the previous chapter, crucifixion was a form of public execution intended, like the sculpture depicting the death of a barbarian warrior, to deter rebellion and dehumanize any who violated Roman law and authority. Seen in this light, it is very clear why Paul's determination to "preach Christ crucified" was "a stumbling-block to Jews and foolishness to Gentiles" (1 Cor 1:23), and why he himself should be abused as being among "the scum of the earth" (1 Cor 4:13).

Brigitte Kahl, while noting that for the imperial rulers the sight of the crucified was a twin image of *The Dying Gaul*, points out that in Paul's preaching this perception is radically violated and subverted:

Jesus did not die for himself and for his own sins but for our sake (Gal 1:4; 2:20). The polar construct of a superior, righteous, law-abiding, justified Self, standing over against an inferior,

---

5. Brigitte Kahl, "Galatians and the 'Orientalism' of Justification by Faith: Paul among Jews and Muslims," in Christopher Stanley, *Colonized Apostle*, 215. See also Kahl's ground-breaking interpretation of the letter to the Galatians: *Galatians Reimagined: Reading with the Eyes of the Vanquished* (Minneapolis: Fortress, 2010).

unrighteous, lawless, sinful Other, collapses, and with it the law of the dominant order which justifies crucifixion, imperial warfare, and colonial subjugation. The Self can be justified only if it accepts its unjustifiable complicity in the Other's death and thus its own status as sinner.[6]

Furthermore, and this connects with a major theme of this present book, Kahl concludes that the collapse of the Self–Other dichotomy results in a "profound transformation" of the image of God. The religious and political promoters of the imperial order assumed that god or gods were on their side; they were the transcendent guarantors of the way the world was, including the identification of others as lawless and sinful. Paul, by contrast, has recognized that in the crucified Christ God is reimagined on the side of *The Dying Gaul*, so "subverting any notion of God-willed and lawful violence that the Self can impose on the Other for God's sake and in alliance with God." With the justification and liberation of "the sinner, the loser, the defeated" the ideology of victory, conquest and colonization as divinely willed falls apart.[7]

Writing to the Corinthians, Paul recounts the cost of the downward mobility which was the consequence of his confession of Christ and his preaching of the message of the cross throughout the empire: "To this very hour we go hungry and thirsty, we are in rags, we are brutally treated, we are homeless. We work hard with our own hands [manual labour!]. When we are cursed, we bless; when we are persecuted, we endure it; when we are slandered, we answer kindly. Up to this moment *we have become the scum of the earth, the refuse of the world*" (1 Cor 4:11–13). The emphasized phrases indicate the *social* cost of identification both with the crucified Christ and with people at the margins of a highly stratified society who had discovered hope, joy, love

---

6. Kahl, "Galatians," 218. See also David L. Balch, "Paul's Portrait of Christ Crucified (Gal. 3:1) in Light of Paintings and Sculptures of Suffering and Death in Pompeiian and Roman Houses," in *Early Christian Families in Context: An Interdisciplinary Dialogue*, ed. David L. Balch and Carolyn Osiek (Grand Rapids, MI: Eerdmans, 2003), 84–108. At the conclusion of a fascinating discussion of the depiction of suffering in Greek and Roman art, Balch notes that Augustus "portrayed his battles not as civil war but as a conflict of Romans against Eastern barbarians." By contrast, Jewish Christian baptism repudiated such ideology and confessed "that God's call and not ethnic identity determines human worth. . . . Paul's polemical gospel was disturbing because he embodied, proclaimed, and challenged key Roman ideological values" (107–108).

7. Terry Eagleton comments, "In its solidarity with the outcast and the afflicted, the crucifixion is a critique of all hubristic humanism. Only through a confession of loss and failure can the very meaning of power be transfigured in the miracle of the resurrection. The death of God is the life of the iconoclastic Jesus, who shatters the idolatrous image of Yahweh as irascible despot and shows him up instead as vulnerable flesh and blood." *Culture and the Death of God*, 159.

and a previously unheard-of dignity in the good news preached by Paul. In a culture in which honour and shame determined all human interactions and relationships, the reaction of the privileged and powerful to such a movement and to one of its leading promoters was entirely predictable. Paul and his converts counted for nothing; they were the lowest form of human life, or, if slaves, were scarcely recognized as human beings at all. Except, that is, if they together became something other than a minuscule sect with no pretensions to bring about change, in which case social stigma would quickly be followed by repressive measures.

New Testament scholars have pointed out the degrading nature of the phrases Paul cites in these verses. Anthony Thiselton observes that "the scum of the earth" refers to the dirt removed as the result of scouring an unclean vessel, while "the refuse of the world" indicates "the unmentionable dirt that people scrape off their shoes when they wipe them clean."[8] Not to put too fine a point on this, Paul is aware that he and his people are regarded as excrement!

However, I have not been able to find a commentator who sees significance in the fact that exactly the same imagery is found in the book of Lamentations where we find this statement addressed to God:

> You have covered yourself with a cloud
> so that no prayer can get through.
> You have made us scum and refuse
> among the nations. (Lam 3:44–45)

Paul was surely familiar with this text and we may ask whether, by using the very same imagery, he recognized a parallel between the contempt with which the Jewish survivors and exiles had been treated by the imperial power of Babylon, and his own experience, together with that of his converts, in the context of the Roman Empire? And did he see particular significance in the phrase "among the nations," since those same nations now shared Israel's suffering as subjugated and conquered peoples incorporated within the Roman *imperium*? It was precisely among those peoples that he laboured to bring into being a new social reality within which God's promise of *shalom* would be realized.

If the connection I am suggesting here is valid, then it becomes clear that Paul must have needed and employed the language of *lament* in the course of a costly and sacrificial ministry in the context of the imperial power which

---

8. Anthony Thiselton, *1 Corinthians: A Shorter Exegetical and Pastoral Commentary* (Grand Rapids, MI: Eerdmans, 2006), 76–77.

dominated the very peoples to whom the apostle believed he was sent. As Davina Lopez puts it:

> Paul as an apostle who goes down among the defeated nations, has had to come to terms with the ideological configuration designating all others as inferior to Roman rule. In the prophetic new creation Paul is struggling so hard in labor to usher into being, all the nations must turn from idolatry – the civic worship of the one master of the world – and turn as children toward the God of Israel, the creator of the world, who will reconcile them all with one another and end war forever.[9]

The "Wretched Man" of Romans 7

What makes Romans 7 a crucial text for this book is that it is one of the few places within the New Testament where we hear language which clearly echoes the lament as we have found this within the Hebrew Bible. The anguished cry at the heart of this chapter seems, on the surface at least, to express personal distress concerning the unbearable tension between what is promised by the gospel and the reality of life in the context of an ongoing struggle with evil and temptation. Paul seems to confess what may be called "the divided self": "I do not understand what I do. For what I want to do I do not do, *but what I hate I do*" (7:15). The battle to which he refers is not merely spiritual but has psychological and physical dimensions; he says that he delights in the will of God in his "inner being," yet discovers "another law at work *in the members of my body*, waging war against the law of my mind and making me *a prisoner of the law of sin at work within my members*" (7:22–23). The depth of emotional and spiritual pain created by this struggle comes to clear expression in the acknowledgement of the "wretchedness" of this person, leading to the question, "Who will rescue me from this body of death?" (7:24).

Few passages in the New Testament have generated such an enormous amount of debate among scholars as this one! The central issue concerns the identity of the person who speaks here: is Paul confessing his own struggles, and if so, does the experience to which he testifies relate to his life in Christ, or is he recalling the agonized conflict he remembered as characteristic of his pre-conversion life? Clearly, we cannot discuss these issues in detail here, far less claim to be able to resolve the ambiguities and uncertainties which continue

---

9. Lopez, *Apostle to the Conquered*, 150.

to confound commentators.[10] I am inclined to the view that the conflict in question is that of Paul himself and that it is both present and continuing, since, as Ann Jervis observes, the text contains no indication that "Paul has turned his attention away from the description of the Christian life that he began in 3:21, and that he continues to the end of chapter 8."[11]

However, I want to reflect on this text from an angle in which careful attention is given to the broadest context within which Paul lived and worked. That context, as we have seen above, was dominated by an imperial power exercising an influence which seeped into every aspect of life in the ancient world. Paul understood the radically counter-cultural message of the cross and lived this out in practice in his own life to an extraordinary degree, and yet he knew perfectly well the all-pervasive nature of the powerful forces which were embedded within the very structures of his world and which constantly and subtly worked to neutralize the gospel's alternative vision, both within his converts and in his own life.

Paul frequently uses language referring to "powers" which are at work in the very structures of human existence, shaping ideologies, creating worldviews and infiltrating social and cultural systems in ways that determined the shape of the lives of individuals. For example, the institution of *slavery*, which was fundamental to Roman society and lay at the foundation of its economic life, or the cultural system of *honour and shame*, which fixed the status of individuals and locked them into an assigned place within society, were extremely powerful forces which closed down the space for freedom and change.[12] The reality of these "powers" is clear elsewhere in Paul's letter to the Romans in the tensions

---

10. The division between commentators can be illustrated by comparing C. E. B. Cranfield's comments with those of Robert Jewett. Cranfield writes: "The more [Paul] is renewed by God's Spirit, the more sensitive he becomes to the continuing power of sin over his life and the fact that even his very best activities are marred by the egotism still entrenched within him." *Romans*, vol. 1, International Critical Commentary (Edinburgh: T&T Clark, 1975), 342. Jewett, by contrast, concludes a long discussion by saying that the "I" in the text refers to "Paul the zealot prior to his conversion." *Romans: A Commentary*, Hermeneia (Minneapolis: Fortress, 2007), 445.

11. L. Ann Jervis, "Reading Romans 7 in Conversation with Postcolonial Theory: Paul's Struggle toward a Christian Identity of Hybridity," in Christopher Stanley, *Colonized Apostle*, 99.

12. Peter Oakes has imagined a Roman house church which includes among its members a slave named "Iris" who "is constrained to do things that she dislikes and disapproves of." For her, as for other believing slaves, the urgent question which arose again and again would be how the claim to be "no longer enslaved to sin" could be reconciled to the reality that they remained "physically enslaved to the owner" who could demand actions which troubled the renewed conscience? Oakes concludes: "Much of the freeing of the body is yet to come. A sexually exploited slave such as Iris recognizes this well. An 'over-realized' eschatology . . . would cut little ice with her, as with many in similar situations since then." *Reading Romans in Pompeii: Paul's Letter at Ground Level* (London: SPCK, 2009), 144, 149.

between Jews and Gentiles and the hostile relationship between the "strong" and the "weak." These differences, which threatened to destroy the distinctive nature of the new community in Christ, had their origins in cultural forces operative within the wider society, the very world within which Paul's converts had been socialized and where they continued to live their everyday lives. When Romans chapter 7 is read with this context in mind, Paul's distress at the abiding power of sin is seen to concern a struggle not only with what lies *within* the individual, but also with those *external* forces which shape consciousness, will and desire, and entice the disciples of Christ to compromise for the sake of social peace, public esteem and personal satisfaction.

At this point we begin to recognize a connection between this chapter and our own lives as people of faith in the context of a globalized world in which cultural forces are at work which are so powerful as to appear practically irresistible. Jane Collier and Rafael Esteban have described human cultures as being both "symbolic" and "diabolic"; on the one hand they unite, sustain and may bring joy and well-being, but on the other, they are capable of becoming the agents of death and destruction, of "institutionalizing oppression and injustice" and "banning dreams and dreamers [and] stoning and crucifying prophets." In the world of the twenty-first century a *culture of economism* has spread across the globe, so that values derived from an economistic worldview have come to shape "our understanding, our evaluations, and our aspirations, and hence [condition] our actions."[13]

In a remarkable piece of work Collier, who is a professional economist, has correlated the experience Paul describes in Romans 7 with the struggles of Christians in a globalized era to allow the gospel to shape their lives in a truly radical manner. She links the struggle of this passage with Paul's discussions of the "powers" elsewhere (Gal 4:2–4; Col 2:8, 16–33) and concludes that the problem of the "wretched man" cannot be simply the result of "weakness of will" but concerns the "cosmic elements central to his own thought system – 'powers of the world' – which enslave created man even though he delights in God's law and tries to fulfil it."[14]

In Paul's first-century world, those "powers" worked through the political, military, religious and social structures of the Roman Empire, whereas in our times the parallel to "slavery to the law" is discovered in "the mind-set imposed by our own presuppositions, ruled by the values of our culture, swayed

---

13. Jane Collier and Rafael Esteban, *From Complicity to Encounter: The Church and the Culture of Economism* (Harrisburg, PA: Trinity Press International, 1998), 10.

14. Jane Collier, *The Culture of Economism: An Exploration of Barriers to Faith-As-Praxis* (Frankfurt: Peter Lang, 1990), 53. Notice the significance of the subtitle!

by the norms of our group," often leaving us bewildered "by organisational requirements to act on the basis of decisions which we did not make." *We do that which we do not want to do!*

Collier's response to this situation is to propose that we need to revisit the subject of *conversion* which she describes as "the reality of redemption experienced in our lives, not merely as a purely religious event or process . . . but also as central to every aspect of thought and action."[15] In a rich discussion of conversion she describes this as an experience which brings about transformation on many levels of existence. For example, *intellectual* conversion enables us "to see the world in new ways" and results in "a fundamental questioning of the basic premises on which all scientific endeavour is conducted in both the natural and social sciences."[16] At the same time there is a *moral* dimension to biblical conversion which "entails the adoption of a value nexus which is consciously and reflectively chosen." The foundation of this moral transformation is discovered in the life of Jesus and demands "a radical adoption of gospel values by the disciple." In the contemporary world this is the point at which conversion creates significant tensions with the dominant culture because "the message of the kingdom involves a 'deconditioning' process, whereby we shed the values we previously held, and adopt those of the gospel."

As an economist Jane Collier has an acute awareness of the nature of the cultural clash which conversion brings about. The values underlying all modern thinking about economic life and human well-being are founded on *self-interest*.

> The point is that the advocacy of selfishness as an instrumental value is totally at variance with the demands of the Gospel. Moral conversion must entail a rejection of the most fundamental of all economic values, and an adoption of what is normally considered to be the non-rational or irrational – a commitment to the welfare of others rather than the self.[17]

Have we perhaps reached the point in this discussion at which the nature of the struggle of Romans 7 can be seen a little more clearly, while recognizing that our own context in a world being wholly reshaped by the forces of globalization is one in which we discover our own "wretchedness" and the painful failures to claim the freedom which is ours in Christ? Which of us, when reflecting

---

15. Collier, *Culture of Economism*, 287.

16. Collier, 304.

17. Collier, 313.

on the Laodicean compromises of contemporary Christianity, the creeping accommodation to the totalitarian demands of Mammon and the surrender to rising tides of exclusivism and nationalism, will not recognize and identify with Paul's sense of anguish? Even more to the point, must we not confess our chronic underestimation of the strength of the forces hostile to our faith and holiness, and with the apostle renew our hope and trust in Jesus Christ our Lord?

In a slim, popular commentary on Romans, Robert Jewett concludes his notes on chapter 7 with words which suggest that commentators may sometimes reach similar conclusions by different routes:

> The hope for which Paul gives thanks . . . is particularly relevant for persons and nations that discover contradictions between ideals and performance in their own history. Christ alone can deliver us from the past. His life and death reveal the essence of our dilemma. They convey to us an acceptance at so profound a level that we are able to accept ourselves as we are. Then we can cease the sinful striving to be the centre of the world. This chapter is as relevant to individuals as it is to nations. Thanks be to God![18]

Like a Mother in Pain

In a quotation earlier in this chapter Davina Lopez mentioned Paul's statement that he was "struggling . . . in labor" to bring into being a new creation, a human family no longer divided, warring and resentful, but reconciled and united in love and mutual respect. That phrase is perhaps the most remarkable of all the images he uses to describe himself and his mission. It occurs in his address to the Galatians as "My dear children, for whom I am again *in the pains of childbirth until Christ is formed in you* . . . " (Gal 4:19). This is not the only occasion on which Paul deploys this kind of subversive metaphor since, in what is probably his earliest letter, he reminds the Thessalonians that "we were gentle among you, *like a mother caring for her little children*" (1 Thess 2:7). This is surprising language in the context of a rigidly patriarchal culture and it clearly has relevance to the issue of gender roles, both within Paul's first-century Mediterranean context and in the world in which we live today. We might perhaps suggest that Paul here provides us with glimpses of the manner in which his radical claim that in Christ there is "neither male nor

---

18. Robert Jewett, *Romans*, Basic Bible Commentary (Nashville: Abingdon Press, 1988), 90.

female" actually works out in practice, both in leadership within the believing community and, more broadly, in family and social life. This text also indicates the extraordinary transformation which has taken place within this person, from being blinded by a racial pride and prejudice which drove him to acts of violence in the name of religion, to a man who now behaves in a manner which transgresses gender stereotypes and celebrates *gentleness* among converts who had "become so dear to us" (2:8). As Lopez says, the progression from "conquering male, to conquered male identified with conquered people, to labouring mother" is extraordinary and results in a "loss of status and the creation of something new from below."[19]

In using the metaphor of a woman enduring the pain of childbirth, Paul dramatically illustrates the emotional and spiritual (and perhaps physical) agonies which his own mission involved. Childbirth in the ancient world was both far more public and more dangerous than today, and life and death often came together, for both mother and child. In the densely crowded tenements of a city like Rome, the screams of women desperately seeking to bring a child to birth would often have been heard, doubtless accompanied by anguished cries to heaven which may well have taken the form of lament. Consequently, if we take Paul's language seriously we are bound to conclude that the seemingly endless struggle to bring into existence communities of faith in which signs of the arrival of the kingdom of God were evident involved personal pain and distress in which the prayer of lament, so familiar from his own tradition, must have been frequently uttered.

The texts we have briefly examined all suggest that something similar to the dialectic between a "core testimony" of faith and a "counter-testimony" arising from the ambiguities of history, which we have seen to be characteristic of the experience of biblical Israel, can be discerned in the life of Paul. In his case, the extraordinary extent of his vision of the transformation to be wrought by the gospel of the crucified Christ was bound to be challenged by a world held in the grip of an ideology which took the form of a political religion backed up by immense legal and military power. Indeed, Paul's biography reveals the dissonance between the boundless extent of the hope he expresses when writing to the followers of Jesus in Rome and the harsh reality of the end of his ministry as a chained prisoner of the empire facing almost certain death on charges of "treason."[20]

---

19. Lopez, *Apostle to the Conquered*, 146.

20. With regard to "the boundless extent of Paul's hope," see appendix 1, which expands on Paul's missionary theology.

"Remember My Chains"

The subject of Paul's imprisonments and the relationship between those experiences and his letters to the churches is complex and difficult and we cannot engage in discussion of the many disputed details concerning this matter.[21] What is beyond dispute is that the apostle to the Gentiles "was imprisoned many times and for long periods."[22] The picture Luke has given us at the end of the book of Acts seems almost to make light of imprisonment in Nero's Rome and so presents us with the "heroic Paul" we have mentioned earlier, but the apostle's own correspondence while chained to Roman soldiers offers a different perspective from which we discover the harsh realities of "torture, hunger, nakedness, anxiety, and distress in his numerous experiences of prison (1 Thess 2:2; 1 Cor 4:9–13; 2 Cor 6:4–5; 11:23–27; 12:10)."[23]

At the end of his ministry Paul was confined in Rome awaiting a verdict which he knew could bring the death penalty. This suggests that he had been charged with the crime of *maiestas*, or "treason." If this seems puzzling on the basis of our reading of the apostle's letters we need to understand the context in which people might be charged with disloyalty to the imperial rulers for actions or words that appear to us to be completely innocent. During the reign of Nero a fanatical jealousy for the emperor's honour led to prosecutions on the flimsiest of grounds, as a case described by Apollonius shows. Nero composed songs and hired a minstrel to sing them in public, and anyone mocking these performances or speaking ill of the compositions was liable to arrest and the charge of dishonouring the emperor. "A drunken fellow . . . was in the habit of going round about Rome singing Nero's songs and hired for the purpose, and anyone who neglected to listen to him or refused to pay him for his music, he had the right to arrest for violating Nero's *majesty*."[24]

For what reason might Paul have incurred the suspicion and wrath of the imperial authorities? As we know, some of his letters were written during his imprisonments, including the epistle to the Philippians which, in the opinion

---

21. For information on various reconstructions of Paul's life and times and the dating of his letters, see Calvin Roetzel's helpful charts of a series of attempts to plot key events in the apostle's life in his *Paul: The Man and the Myth* (Edinburgh: T&T Clark, 1999), 178–183.

22. Angela Standhartinger, "Letter from Prison as Hidden Transcript: What It Tells Us about the People at Philippi," in *The People beside Paul: The Philippian Assembly and History from Below*, ed. Joseph Marchal (Atlanta: SBL, 2015), 108.

23. Standhartinger, "Letter from Prison," 110.

24. Quoted in Richard J. Cassidy, *Paul in Chains: Roman Imprisonment and the Letters of St. Paul* (New York: Crossroad, 2001), 62.

of a number of scholars, was sent from confinement in Rome.[25] This letter, despite being described by some commentators as "an epistle of joy," is full of references to Paul's difficult situation; no fewer than four times in the opening verses he says "I am in chains," and there is evidence of both deep uncertainty (1:20–26) and profound sorrow and anxiety (2:25–30).

No letter written in such circumstances was likely to remain private between sender and receiver but would have been intercepted, carefully scrutinized for signs of subversion, and might well have placed the addressees under pressure. As Angela Standhartinger says, letter-writing while incarcerated on a capital charge in Nero's Rome "demanded a degree of ambiguity in speaking and writing that has made difficulty for interpreters of Philippians from then until now, for a letter written in prison *must reckon with being read by more than the immediate addressees, namely, by prison guards, police personnel, and judges.*"[26]

The problems in deciphering Paul's meanings can be illustrated in a passage at the heart of his argument where he launches a fierce critique against "the enemies of the cross of Christ." According to the usual translation, such people have made their *bellies* their god and have gloried in what should be to their *shame* (Phil 3:19). The obscurity surrounding this text for modern Western scholars is illustrated by the acknowledgement of Gordon Fee that "in terms of specifics, we are largely in the dark."[27] The same thing might be said with regard to many statements throughout the Pauline correspondence since, as Neil Elliott has said, we tend to assume that we know Paul's meaning when the truth is that we "are constantly reminded of how much *we do not know.*"[28] Does that uncertainty arise, at least in part, because in the original context Paul was compelled by circumstances to *conceal* his message, to write in a kind of

---

25. Among the reasons which Gordon Fee cites for accepting the tradition that Philippians was written from prison in Rome is the statement that it had become clear "throughout the whole palace [Praetorian] guard . . . that I am in chains for Christ" (1:13). This statement clearly implies "that Paul is incarcerated in Rome." *Philippians*, IVP New Testament Commentary (Downers Grove, IL: InterVarsity Press, 1999), 33.

26. Standhartinger, "Letter from Prison," 113; emphasis added.

27. Fee, *Philippians*, 163.

28. Neil Elliott, "Strategies of Resistance and Hidden Transcripts in the Pauline Communities," in *Hidden Transcripts and the Arts of Resistance: Applying the Work of James C. Scott to Jesus and Paul*, ed. Richard A. Horsley (Atlanta: SBL, 2004), 102. Elliott goes on to say that "economic pressures on the urban poor gathered in various first-century Roman cities were stark, and mass violence a regular occurrence." The accounts of Augustus's victories suggest the "social dislocation and economic disruption that military conquest, mass enslavements, and the 'globalization' of the economy (i.e., the assimilation of local economies into the imperial economy) must have occasioned" (104).

code which the Philippians would understand, while circumventing the danger posed by the imperial censors?

The possibility that this is one source of our difficulties in interpretation is increased if we accept the explanation of Richard Cassidy that Paul's primary concern in the passage mentioned above is with "the Roman ethos of licentiousness which surrounds the Philippian Christians" and is "highly hostile to the sexual morality envisioned by the Christian gospel." According to Cassidy, Paul is concerned with sexual ethics at a time when the ruling elite paraded their lusts in patterns of public behaviour in which the desires of the flesh were indulged without restraint or control.[29] *Paul's primary focus, then, is not, as has been widely assumed, Jewish evangelists who seek to impose a new legalism upon the Philippians, but rather is directed toward "the Roman ethos of licentiousness" which pervaded both the city to which the letter was addressed and, to an even greater degree, the imperial capital from which it was sent. Cassidy argues that the obscure phrase "their god is their kolia" has nothing to do with the "belly" but is a euphemism for the male sex organ. The scandal is not obesity but the fact that they worship their penises!* Pornographic imagery, including depictions of the phallus, was ubiquitous in the Graeco-Roman cities and the sexual excesses of the imperial elite in Rome were often noted with disgust by Roman writers. Here is Tacitus describing Nero's behaviour:

> On the quays of the lake stood brothels, filled with women of high rank; and opposite, naked harlots met the view. First came obscene gestures and dances, then as darkness advanced, the whole neighbouring grove, together with the dwelling-houses around, began to echo with song and glitter with lights. Nero himself, defiled by every natural and unnatural lust, had left no abomination in reserve with which to crown his vicious existence.[30]

If the letter to the Philippians was written from Rome the possibility that an imperial agent acting on behalf of Nero realized the subversive nature of

---

29. Cassidy, *Paul in Chains*, 170.

30. Quoted in Cassidy, 147. Howard Marshall agrees that *kolia* "can be used euphemistically for the sexual organ," but then concludes that Paul implies that circumcision has become an idol! See Mark D. Nanos's discussion of the readership of the letter to the Philippians, "Out-Howling the Cynics: Reconceptualizing the Concerns of Paul's Audience from His Polemics in Philippians 3," in Marchal, *People beside Paul*, 183–221.

its subtext is entirely plausible.[31] And what if something similar may be true with regard to the earlier letter Paul had written to the followers of Jesus in the imperial capital, including those living in the squalid tenement blocks of Trastevere? Was the letter to the Romans intercepted and its announcement of the wrath of God against "the godlessness and wickedness of men who suppress the truth by their wickedness" recognized as directed against the hubris of the dominant classes in Rome? Paul's hearers living on the underside of the very city which had witnessed the savagery and debauchery of one Caesar after another would have heard many of his phrases as *allusions* to the imperial household and every detail of Romans 1:18–32 could be read as an accurate description "of the misdeeds of one or another recent member of the Julio-Claudian dynasty."[32] If the Roman authorities cracked the code of this letter, so that the hidden transcript which, for example, urged poor people at the margins of society to "not conform any longer to the pattern of this world" but to be transformed, to *think for themselves* and to "test and approve what God's will is" (12:1–2), then Paul's fate was sealed. Little wonder that he testifies to "being poured out like a drink offering" and acknowledges that he has known "sorrow upon sorrow" together with the temptation to anxiety (Phil 2:17, 27–28).

The Precarious Vision

It has been said that the opposite of faith is not doubt, but certainty. I wish to argue that the truth of that statement can be seen in the life of the apostle Paul in which the interaction between praise and lament so characteristic of biblical religion can be traced in the "confessional" statements we have discussed in this chapter. Paul's understanding of the significance of the life,

---

31. Dieter Georgi believes that Philippians was written during an earlier imprisonment in Ephesus, but his comments are relevant here: "Because he is in the hands of the Romans and therefore in immediate political danger, he has to be careful and change his tone." He suggests that the description of the exaltation of Jesus in 2:6–11 would have suggested to the original hearers the events which followed the deaths of Roman emperors who were proclaimed to have known "heavenly assumption and apotheosis by resolution of the Roman senate, ratified in heaven." By contrast, the death "that makes Jesus the first among equals and equal to the biblical God is suffered neither in battle nor on a sickbed, but on a Roman cross." Georgi concludes: "no Roman censor would think it necessary to fear a crucified pretender. . . . He would rank such a notion as an absurdity. *In this fashion, nevertheless, Paul launches a critical infiltration of the reigning political and social principles.*" *Theocracy in Paul's Praxis and Theology* (Minneapolis: Fortress, 1991), 72–74; emphasis added.

32. Neil Elliott, *The Arrogance of Nations: Reading Romans in the Shadow of Empire* (Minneapolis: Fortress, 2008), 82.

death and resurrection of Christ was truly *revolutionary*, both in the sense that he recognized that the ancient promises of the Hebrew prophets of a time of renewal, encapsulated in the promise of *shalom*, were actually being fulfilled in his lifetime, and in that this radical message challenged the entire foundations of the existing world order shaped by the imperial ideology of the Roman Empire. As Tom Wright says, within the first generation of the Jesus movement "there was an explosion of revolutionary beliefs about what had been achieved on the day Jesus died" and the resultant revolution "had a definite shape that remained constant across different traditions and widely different styles of expression."[33]

Nonetheless, as we have seen, the great vision of a world transformed, of nations and peoples reconciled and freed from oppression, and of the creation itself healed and liberated from bondage, remained the object of *hope* as the empires of this world revealed a depressing staying power and repeatedly persuaded the followers of Jesus to abandon the revolutionary core of their religion. Paul himself clearly recognized this tension, reminding the Roman believers that they were *saved in hope* and that, despite the conviction that the "age to come" had broken into the present, believers continued to "hope for what we do not yet have" (Rom 8:24–25). While the pastoral advice to "wait patiently" for a future consummation of the kingdom of God is important, there is at the same time a holy *impatience* with the apparent failure of the gospel to fulfil its promises and with the depressing regularity with which the followers of Jesus have diluted his message, suppressed its ethical imperatives and reached comfortable forms of accommodation with the world he came to save.

While the tension between "now" and "not yet" was familiar to Paul throughout his ministry, I suggest that it must have been particularly acute during his last confinement in Rome. Some years earlier he had told the Christ-followers in the imperial capital that his great ambition was to reach the western end of the known world in order to make the message of the cross known to the peoples of Spain (Rom 15:23–24). Indeed, according to Robert Jewett, the entire letter to the Romans "was designed to prepare the ground for the complicated project of the Spanish mission, including the insistence that the impartial righteousness of God does not discriminate against 'barbarians' such as the Spaniards." Paul was clearly aware of tensions within the Christian community at Rome and of differences of opinion concerning himself and his ministry. As Jewett says, the apostle exposes all claims to cultural superiority as bogus and

---

33. Wright, *Day the Revolution Began*, 350.

argues that imperial propaganda is false, while "the domineering behavior of congregations toward one another must be overcome *if the missional hope to unify the world in the praise of God is to be fulfilled* (15:9–13)."[34]

Some years later Paul finally arrived in the city of Rome, but the great missionary vision which had loomed so large at the conclusion of his earlier letter had by this time turned into a dream never likely to become reality. Paul had himself put this great project to one side in order that he might prioritize the completion of his obligation to his own, Jewish people (15:25–28). He had previously unequivocally affirmed his Jewish identity, describing the people of Israel as "my brothers, those of my own race," and he acknowledged that their unbelief caused him "great sorrow and unceasing anguish in my heart" (9:2–3). The language suggests a deep and abiding emotional and spiritual distress, so that the pain Paul describes "is neither superficial nor transitory but remains with him as a chronic condition."[35] We will not discuss the significance of the delivery of the "collection" to the Jewish followers of Messiah Jesus in Jerusalem at this point except to say that Paul's journey back to Palestine was motivated by his passionate love for his own people, and by the deep conviction that the reconciling power of the cross had destroyed the barriers which divided peoples from each other and made possible a new unity-in-diversity within the one body of Christ. Consequently, however great the desire might have been to reach Spain and preach where Christ was not known, *the unity of the new people of God, both Jew and Gentile, had to be a visible, public reality if Paul's proclamation at the new frontiers of mission was to have credibility.* So crucial was this issue for Paul that he was willing to risk not only the mission in the West but his very own life and freedom in the attempt to overcome the tensions threatening to destroy the unity of the *ekklesia* of Christ.

Consider, then, Paul's state of mind when he arrived as a chained prisoner in Nero's Rome. The risky journey back to the seething cauldron of Jerusalem had ended in his arrest, and the hope that the "collection" might act as a catalyst to unify the Jesus movement and display to the world the reconciling power of the cross lay in tatters. One commentator has concluded that the entire collection effort had proved disastrous since Paul's presence in Jerusalem "with representatives of the Gentile churches was a provocation to some faction in the Jewish community."[36] Worse still, the very same issues which had surfaced

---

34. Jewett, *Romans: A Commentary*, Hemeneia, 79; emphasis added.

35. Jewett, 559.

36. Wayne Meeks, *The First Urban Christians: The Social World of the Apostle Paul* (New Haven: Yale University Press, 1983), 110.

in Jerusalem were now creating renewed tensions between the believing communities within the city of Rome itself. If the Philippian letter was written during this final imprisonment, its reference to some who suppose "that they can stir up trouble for me while I am in chains" (Phil 1:17) suggests that a long-standing reluctance to accept Paul's ministry on the part of a minority had spilled over into active opposition and a refusal to identify with a man facing the charge of treason in Nero's Rome! Cassidy points out that Paul probably arrived in the imperial capital shortly after Nero had murdered his own mother and a few years before he was to launch a vicious assault upon the followers of Jesus in Rome, bringing martyrdom and great suffering to them.

> Presumably, in the eyes of a minority of Roman Christians, Paul's status as a prisoner and the chains he wore were a profound embarrassment. Indeed, for this minority, it was not tolerable that the prisoner Paul be taken as *the* authoritative exponent of Christ *in Rome*. These Christians had antedated Paul in Rome by many years and they had built up their community life, working out their own *modus vivendi* regarding the imperial authorities.[37]

When Paul refers to the experience of "sorrow upon sorrow" (Phil 2:27) he might have been describing the double blow of the failure of his visit to Jerusalem, followed by the realization that his chains now isolated him from those followers of Jesus in Rome who feared that any publicly expressed sympathy toward someone charged with treason would place them in peril. As Cassidy says, association with someone being watched day and night by the Praetorian Guard "could pose dangers for the whole conclave of Christians now present in Rome" who feared that they might "be brought to such chains."[38]

In the letter Paul had written to the Romans he had dealt at length with the reality of suffering and loss. He depicted the entire creation as *groaning* under the burden of its abuse and exploitation, and then described the believer's experience as one which involved the sharing of such agonies and "groaning inwardly" as a result of the dissonance between what has been promised by

---

37. Cassidy, *Paul in Chains*, 134. For the best part of half a century Richard Cassidy has done as much as any New Testament scholar to alert us to the imperial context of this entire body of literature. See, in addition to the title cited here, his *Jesus, Politics and Society: A Study in Luke's Gospel* (Maryknoll, NY: Orbis, 1978); *Society and Politics in the Acts of the Apostles* (Maryknoll, NY: Orbis, 1987); *John's Gospel in New Perspective: Christology and the Realities of Roman Power* (Maryknoll, NY: Orbis, 1992); 2nd ed. with new chapter "Johannine Footwashing and Roman Slavery" (Eugene, OR: Wipf & Stock, 2015); and *Christians and Roman Rule in the New Testament: New Perspectives* (New York: Crossroad, 2001).

38. Cassidy, *Paul in Chains*, 134.

the gospel and the reality of facing "death all day long" (Rom 8:20–23, 36). The description of Christians "groaning inwardly" *sounds remarkably like the prayers of lament we have discussed earlier in this book*, and it suggests once again that the tradition of honest spirituality bequeathed to us by the Hebrew Bible is a precious gift to be received with thankfulness by Christians in a world still tragically broken. Elsewhere, Paul confesses that the extreme hardships he faced resulted in "great pressure, far beyond our ability to endure" (2 Cor 1:8). In the light of his subsequent experience, as we have just described this, he may well have come to feel that the burden of suffering and disappointment was to grow to even greater proportions by the end of his life.

However, *something had changed with the crucifixion of Jesus*, so while not in any way minimizing the reality of the depth of Christian suffering, Paul can remind the Romans that the death and resurrection of Jesus has moved us to a place beyond Job where we can say, "If God is for us, who can be against us?" (Rom 8:31). The claim that "God is for us" moves far beyond a conventional theological assertion in that the relationship between God and the suffering world has been totally transformed by the cross. God is "for us" in the sense that he has known the suffering of this world, reaching down to the very deepest depths of humiliation, pain and loneliness, so displaying a love from which nothing "in all creation" can separate us (8:39)! In the cross of Jesus Christ the anguished, angry cries of the sufferers of all the ages find a response which not only offers a ground for hope in our broken world, but – as we shall see in the next chapter – brings about a change in God himself.

For Reflection

If I speak with the eloquence of men and of angels, but have no love, I become no more than blaring brass or crashing cymbal. If I have the gift of foretelling the future and hold in my mind not only all human knowledge but the very secrets of God, and if I also have that absolute faith that can move mountains, but have no love, I amount to nothing at all. If I dispose of all that I possess, yes, even if I give my own body to be burned, but have no love, I achieve precisely nothing.

This love of which I speak is slow to lose patience – it looks for a way to be constructive. It is not possessive: it is neither anxious to impress nor does it cherish inflated ideas of its own importance.

Love has good manners and does not pursue selfish advantage. It is not touchy. It does not keep an account of evil or gloat over the wickedness of other people. On the contrary, it is glad with all good people when truth prevails.

Love knows no limit to its endurance, no end to its trust, no fading of its hope; it can outlast anything. It is, in fact, the one thing that still stands when all else has fallen.

For if there are prophecies they will be fulfilled and done with, if there are "tongues" the need for them will disappear, if there is knowledge it will be swallowed up in truth. For our knowledge is always incomplete, and when the complete comes, that is the end of the incomplete.

When I was a little child I talked and felt and thought like a child. Now that I am a man my childish speech and feeling and thought have no further significance for me.

At present we are people looking at puzzling reflections in a mirror. The time will come when we shall see reality whole and face to face! At present all I know is a little fraction of the truth, but the time will come when I shall know as fully as God now knows me! In this life we have three great lasting qualities – faith, hope and love. But the greatest of them is love.[39]

---

39. 1 Cor 13 in J. B. Phillips, *The New Testament in Modern English* (London: Geoffrey Bles, 1960), 364–365.

Christ calls people to bring the divine ideal to reality. Only short-sighted people imagine that Christianity has already happened, that it took place in, say, the thirteenth century, or the fourth, or some other time. I would say that it has only made the first hesitant steps in the history of the human race. Many words of Christ are still incomprehensible to us even now, because we are still Neanderthals in spirit and morals; because the arrow of the gospel is aimed at eternity; because the history of Christianity is only beginning. What has happened already, what we now call the history of Christianity, are the first half-clumsy, unsuccessful attempts to make it a reality.[40]

---

40. This passage comes from the final address of the great Russian Orthodox priest Alexander Men and was spoken in September 1990 on the evening before his brutal murder. See "Christianity for the Twenty-First Century," in *Christianity for the Twenty-First Century: The Life and Work of Alexander Men*, ed. Elizabeth Roberts and Ann Shukman (London: SCM, 1996), 185.

5

Speaking of God

Christianity is the only religion on earth that has felt
omnipotence made God incomplete.
—G. K. Chesterton

Having traced the origin and development of the tradition of lament
through the Bible it is clear that what distinguishes this form of prayer
from that which centres on praise and thanksgiving is its *honesty* before God
in voicing doubt concerning the reliability of the divine promises and, more
seriously, its *boldness* in questioning the relationship between the Almighty
and the recurrent tragedies in human history, including those which afflict his
devout worshippers. Lament moves the practice of prayer beyond a passive
acceptance of whatever life brings upon us and raises questions which require
answers. In doing so, lament seeks to initiate a *dialogue* with heaven, hoping –
longing – that God will respond to the sufferer's anguish and confusion.

For example, the dilemma of Job arises from the fact that while he confesses
the absolute sovereignty of God, acknowledging that "His wisdom is profound,
his power is vast" (9:4), this core belief runs into an insurmountable barrier
when he attempts to relate it to the catastrophe of invasion or the suffering of
the poor in a corrupt society:

When a scourge brings sudden death,
> he mocks the despair of the innocent.
When a land falls into the hands of the wicked,
> he blindfolds its judges.
If it is not he, then who is it? (9:23–24)

Clearly, this is *not* a question arising from unbelief; on the contrary, it is asked
from within a theistic faith at the point at which the believer's most cherished
convictions become the source of an insoluble dilemma. Job's agonized

question is not the commencement of a path which leads to atheism, but a quest for a new knowledge of God which might provide an alternative to the image of an unfeeling tyrant or a celestial puppet master who plays cruel games with individuals and nations. Job's dilemma has enormous resonance today, as Albert Camus realized when wrestling with the moral crisis of an age of total war in 1942:

> In the presence of God there is less a problem of freedom than a problem of evil. You know the alternative: either we are not free and God the all-powerful is responsible for evil. Or we are free and responsible but God is not all-powerful. All the scholastic subtleties have neither added nor subtracted anything from the acuteness of this paradox.[1]

Notice that Camus assumes that Christian theism involves a belief that God is "all-powerful." This is hardly surprising since the confession of divine *omnipotence* has indeed been central to both theology and worship for centuries, resulting in a piety which acknowledged and submitted to God's will even in the most profoundly tragic of circumstances, as did Job himself at an early stage in his story (1:20–21). However, in contrast to the Bible, which clearly permits the questioning of God's justice and contains evidence that there are dangerous cracks in the doctrine of divine omnipotence, Western theology became trapped within a tradition which had parted company with the biblical narrative at certain critical points. As a result, by the twentieth century, scarred, as we have seen, by violence and destruction on a previously unimaginable scale, those cracks opened up in a way that was to result in the collapse of religion throughout post-war Europe. The form of theism inherited from the age of Christendom became increasingly incredible in the face of the horrors of two world wars, the genocide associated with names like Bergen-Belsen and Auschwitz, and the mushroom clouds over the ruins of Hiroshima and Nagasaki. At the time few Christians in Europe recognized the seriousness of the crisis facing the churches, but the Dutch theologian J. C. Hoekendijk provided a dramatic example of the shift occurring in Western culture, quoting

---

1. Albert Camus, *The Myth of Sisyphus* (London: Penguin, 1975; originally published as *Le Mythe de Sisyphe* in 1942), 55. Camus felt this dilemma to be insoluble and it led him to speak of the *absurdity of the world*. "I don't know whether this world has a meaning that transcends it. But I know that I do not know that meaning and that it is impossible for me to know it just now. . . . And these two certainties – my appetite for the absolute and for unity and the impossibility of reducing this world to a rational and reasonable principle – I also know that I cannot reconcile them" (51).

the words of a returned prisoner of war traumatized by his experiences in Russia and seeking solace in the church:

> There is a preacher talking from behind the pulpit. We don't understand him. A glass cover has been put over the pulpit. This smothers all sound. Around the pulpit our contemporaries are standing. They too talk, and they call. But on the inside this is not understood. The glass cover smothers all sound. Thus, we still *see* each other talk, but we don't understand each other anymore.[2]

Could there be a more vivid picture of the breakdown in communication between a church deploying theological language which had become tired and devoid of relevance and a generation recovering from the traumas of mechanized warfare, asking serious questions which went largely unheard or misunderstood? Above all, the issue at stake concerned the very being of God and his relationship to the ghastly horrors of a continent devastated by death and destruction and by the revelation of the depths of depravity to which human beings might descend. As Terence Fretheim comments, traditional images of God were disconnected from common human experience and seemed "to float above the maelstrom of actual life" or were "narrowly associated with one or another segment of society."[3]

Lost in Translation

In the previous chapter we discussed the burning passion of the apostle Paul to preach Christ among the nations, a task which demanded the linguistic and cultural translation of the message of the gospel in order that it might be heard as good news in the context of the Graeco-Roman world. Paul thus initiated the first great cross-cultural transmission of the Christian faith in history, a process which resulted in a plurality of expressions of the religion. However, with the destruction of the city of Jerusalem in 70 CE the original Jewish, messianic followers of Jesus were scattered and the centre of gravity of the growing Christian movement shifted to the Gentile world. As a result, Hellenistic modes of thought came to dominate preaching and theology, eventually eclipsing the Hebrew foundations of the faith in significant respects.

This missionary expansion of the Christian movement arose from an imperative within the gospel itself and resulted in the enrichment of the

---

2. J. C. Hoekendijk, *The Church Inside Out* (London: SCM, 1967), 50.

3. Terence Fretheim, *The Suffering of God: An Old Testament Perspective* (Philadelphia: Fortress, 1984), 16.

tradition as Christ was embraced and understood from within the receiving culture. In other words, converts whose lives were profoundly shaped by the Hellenistic worldview discovered Jesus as the Redeemer of *their* world and contributed new insights which deepened the meaning of the Christ-event. At the same time, there was the possibility that something of crucial importance might be lost in the process of translation as the original Hebrew setting of the tradition was largely forgotten and eventually superseded. As Scott Ellington points out, among the most significant Greek ideas to reshape Christian thought and belief the philosophical concept of *perfection* implied the absence of change, and when God came to be perceived through these cultural and philosophical lenses his character began to be understood in ways which were very different from the testimonies of the Hebrew prophets.[4]

Aristotle had famously described God as the "unmoved Mover," a transcendent Being "completely separate from all that he creates; perfect, eternal, unchangeable, and wholly unaffected by his interaction with humanity."[5] When this image of God began influencing theology there followed a series of consequences which were to reshape the way Christians understood the person of Jesus Christ, the relationship between the physical body and the soul, and the importance assigned to rational thought. By the third century the North African theologian Tertullian could say that since God the Father was without passions he could "not suffer with the Son"; God was "unable to suffer with another as the Son is unable to suffer in virtue of His divinity." Much later in the history of Western Christianity we discover Thomas Aquinas struggling to reconcile the biblical tradition concerning the love and compassion of God with the inherited theology which insisted on the divine impassability: "Mercy is especially to be attributed to God, provided that it is considered as an effect,

---

4. Catherine Keller describes the "linguistic miracle" of Pentecost as "stunning" the disciples into mission. However, the "ontology of changeless, dispassionate Being, of eternal essence presiding over the 'accidents' of space, time, and becoming, came to preside over the church itself." She asks how *love* could survive such metaphysics, "For what is love, when its relations are unilateral, accidental to the One who loves?" The covenantal Lord of history became "hybridized with the unmoved mover; and soon the sovereign Father of orthodoxy – 'God of power and might' as many of our liturgies still chant – manfully merged with the sovereignty of the state. He spoke the one tongue of Rome." In Catherine Keller, Michael Nausner and Mayra Rivera, eds., *Postcolonial Theologies: Divinity and Empire* (St Louis: Chalice, 2004), 222–223.

5. Ellington, *Risking Truth*, 35. I am grateful for the insights of this book, especially on the topic being discussed here.

not as a feeling of suffering. . . . *It does not belong to God to sorrow over the misery of others.*"[6]

However, a deity unable to feel the misery of others became incredible in the age of aerial warfare, death camps and the atom bomb. In fact, as we have seen earlier in this book, the cracks in this form of theistic belief had become visible in the nineteenth century, resulting in Friedrich Nietzsche's announcement that God was *dead*. It was precisely *this* God who had passed away, a deity whose worship was endlessly intoned in creedal statements which identified him as "the Father almighty." Whatever else Nietzsche intended by his shocking statement, it was indeed true that the image of a God whose primary attribute was omnipotent *power* had become unbelievable and no longer had traction in modern culture.[7] In other words, termites had been eating away at the base of an idol for a very long time before the tragedies of the most violent century in human history finally caused it to topple over!

When that happened and preachers were left speaking largely to themselves, voices were heard suggesting that the dead god had always been far removed from the covenantal Lord known to the Hebrew prophets and to Jesus and Paul. Not surprisingly, some of the most significant of those voices were Jewish and they declared that their understanding of God had, like themselves, been ignored and ridiculed throughout the Christian ages. Abraham Heschel, perhaps the most powerful and eloquent of these witnesses, observed that the spirit of Greek thought hovered over every page of Western philosophy: "The prophets are absent when the philosophers speak about God . . . the basic premises of Western philosophy are derived from Greek rather than Hebrew thinking."[8] The Bible, he said, contains a "sublime answer" to the fundamental questions concerning human life, but modern people

---

6. Ellington, 36; emphasis added. John McGuckin describes how, between the fourth and sixth centuries, Christian thinkers adopted and developed "basic positions that would characterize Christianity for many centuries" and that the foundations of these positions "had been laid down in the cultural movement from Semitic to more overtly Greek forms of thought and expression that accelerated throughout the church of the 2nd and 3rd centuries." "Greek Theology, 4th–6th Centuries," in *The Oxford Companion to Christian Thought: Intellectual, Spiritual and Moral Horizons of Christianity*, ed. Adrian Hastings (Oxford: Oxford University Press, 2000), 278–283.

7. Nietzsche was far from a lone voice in declaring the death of God. Heinrich Heine wrote in 1852: "Our heart is full of pity. It is the old Jehovah himself preparing for death. . . . Can you hear the ringing of the bell? Kneel down, they are bringing the sacraments to a dying God." Quoted in J. P. Stern, *Nietzsche* (London: Fontana/Collins, 1978), 93.

8. Abraham Heschel, *God in Search of Man: A Philosophy of Judaism* (London: Souvenir, 2009 [1955]), 24. Scarcely less influential was the work of Martin Buber who ended his *Prophetic Faith* (1949) with these words: "But the great scattering, which followed the splitting up of the

do not know the question any more. When we turn to the Bible with an empty spirit, moved by intellectual vanity, striving to show our superiority to the text, or as barren souls who go sight-seeing to the words of the prophets, we discover the shells but miss the core. It is easier to enjoy beauty than to sense the holy. To be able to encounter the spirit within the words, *we must learn to crave an affinity with the pathos of God.*[9]

The use of the word "pathos" in relation to God signalled the coming of a massive shift in Western theology as the renewed study of the Hebrew Bible, and especially the prophetic books, was to result in the rediscovery of a deity who knew suffering and weakness. Careful examination of the Old Testament revealed what had been lost in translation; that from the creation narratives, to the sealing of the covenant, and down to the supreme crisis of the loss of Jerusalem and its temple, the God of Israel was profoundly engaged with humankind and its history, deeply moved by a broken relationship, and shared the anguish, pain and tears of those who remained faithful to him.[10] As Fretheim says, the Bible was very clear that if the world is affected by God, the reverse is also true and "God is affected by the world in both positive and negative ways."[11]

God is the transcendent Lord; but God is transcendent not in isolation from the world, but in relationship to the world. . . . God is the Lord of time and history, yet God has chosen to be bound up in the time and history of the world and to be limited thereby. God is unchangeable with respect to the steadfastness of his love and his salvific will for all creatures, yet God does change in the light of what happens in the interaction between God and the world.[12]

---

state and became the essential form of the people, is endowed with the mystery of suffering as with the promise of the God of the sufferers" (New York: Macmillan, 1949), 234.

9. Heschel, *God in Search of Man*, 252; emphasis added.

10. The Puritan commentator Matthew Henry observed that when God is reported to have called to Adam and asked "Where are you?" the question implied that man was lost, not from God's knowledge, but from his fellowship. Commenting on God's promise to exiled Israel, "with great compassion I will gather you" (Isa 54:7–8), Walter Brueggemann says the text indicates a divine "propensity to suffer with and suffer for, to be in solidarity with Israel in its suffering." In this historical moment of supreme crisis for faith, "Yahweh found in Yahweh's own internal life a depth of devotion to the well-being of Israel that was not, until that moment of crisis, available to Yahweh." *Theology of the Old Testament*, 299.

11. Fretheim, *Suffering of God*, 35.

12. Fretheim, 35.

What Heschel had called the "pathos" of God was especially clear in the prophetic books where the terrible anguish of Hosea and Jeremiah reflected, or even embodied, the pain of God. The "confessions" of Jeremiah, which amount to personal laments in which he mourns the impending loss of the beloved city and its people and asks why he had to live and preach at such a time, reflect God's own anguish. These remarkable texts are intended to portray not simply the prophet's personal life, but his life as "an enfleshment of the life of God."[13]

The voices of Jewish scholars pointing out that Christian thought had for centuries lost contact with crucial aspects of the revelation granted to the Hebrew prophets were to be joined by an ever-growing chorus of converts from Asia, Africa and Latin America whose cultural and religious contexts owed little or nothing to the ancient Graeco-Roman world so that they read the Bible through quite different cultural lenses and in contexts often marked by deep suffering. We referred earlier in this book to the Japanese theologian Kazoh Kitamori who in 1946, with his country broken and devastated, published the book *Theology of the Pain of God*. He defined salvation as the message that "our God enfolds our broken reality," and in a chapter entitled "Pain as the Essence of God" wrote that the Bible shows that pain belongs to God's *eternal* being. "God, who will appear in the ultimate form of his glory, calls himself 'the first and the last, *who died and came to life*,'" so that the cross of Jesus is not external to God "but an act within himself."[14] Kitamori understood perfectly well that his theology represented a *break* from the traditions received from Western Christendom and he regarded this as absolutely necessary if Christianity was to speak meaningfully into the despair and brokenness of a post-war world, especially in the context of Asia. Classical theology had talked about the *essence* of God, referring to his transcendent glory, yet precisely the exalted nature of this concept had become problematic amid the smoking ruins of burned-out cities and the charred corpses of millions of civilians.

> Frankly, no concept is so *remote* from the biblical concept of God as "essence." Those who know God as revealed to Jeremiah and

---

13. Fretheim, 156. Notice in particular the response of God to Jeremiah's confessions in passages like 12:14–17 and 18:7–10. These texts present us with images of God *struggling* to fulfil his promise of *shalom*, not only to Israel but to all the nations on earth. In the New Testament the key passage is Romans 9–11 in which Paul describes a similar struggle in the context of the ambiguities and uncertainties of history. His warning to Gentile followers of Jesus concerning the peril of arrogance in the light of divine election, and the necessity of continuing in "the kindness of God," needs to be heard today in the era of world Christianity. This crucial passage concludes with a magnificent doxology celebrating God's judgements which are "unsearchable" and "his paths beyond tracing out," Rom 11:33–36.

14. Kitamori, *Theology of the Pain of God*, 45.

Paul notice immediately that God defined as "essence" is missing one vital point: his *real* essence, his true heart. The pain of God which Jeremiah saw, the love in the cross which Paul saw – this is the essence of God, this is the heart of God.[15]

If a deity whose essence consists in transcendent glory, unable to feel "the misery of others," is remote from the reality of human suffering, such a God will also be *deaf to the cries for justice in a world in which power is so often used in ways that are oppressive and destructive*. Worse still, when God's defining attributes came to be regarded as omnipotent power and knowledge, the foundation was laid for an *aristocratic* theology which sanctified forms of social and political life reflecting the nature of this omnipotent God. Consequently the power and privileges of kings and princes were placed beyond challenge, while the mass of people were taught to accept their lowly status as divinely appointed in an established, unchangeable order of things.[16] Throughout the second half of the twentieth-century voices like that of Kazoh Kitamori were joined by those of an ever-growing cloud of witnesses from beyond the Western world, rejecting the image of God as the defender of the status quo and creating a global chorus singing new songs.[17]

There is a divine irony in the fact that although the apostle Paul was never able to fulfil his dream of evangelizing Spain, a vast number of Christians speaking the tongues of the Iberian peninsula are now making vital contributions to what has been described as "the Reformation of the Twentieth Century." Among them the voice of the Hispanic historian Justo González is particularly significant, and he has stressed that the influence of Greek philosophy on the theology of Europe was never socio-politically neutral. Yahweh, who heard the cries of slaves and intervened to liberate them

---

15. Kitamori, *Pain of God*, 46. The final chapter of this remarkable book, "The Pain of God and Gospel History," deserves close attention. It describes the contribution which Japanese Christianity might make toward the recovery of the gospel: "Those of us who have been given the land of Japan as the 'boundaries of habitation' will serve God with all our hearts, bearing the sense of pain as we attempt to comprehend the image and view of God. By doing so, one decisive aspect of God's nature, which was overlooked by the Greek churches, will be recovered by the churches of our country" (136). For a more recent study of the interaction between Christianity and Japanese culture see the profoundly moving work of the Japanese artist Makoto Fujimura in *Silence and Beauty: Hidden Faith Born of Suffering* (Downers Grove, IL: InterVarsity Press, 2016).

16. King James I of England (James VI of Scotland) wrote: "Kings are justly called gods, for they exercise a manner or resemblance of divine power on earth." Note Justo González's statement: "Some gods are better dead than alive . . . Therefore, let us not be too hasty in our condemnation of those who say that the 'God' worshipped by much of our civilization is dead. Perhaps that 'God' too is an idol whose day has passed. And perhaps biblical believers ought to rejoice at the funeral of such a god." González, *Mañana*, 89.

17. See appendix 2, "A Global Chorus Singing New Songs."

from oppression, had been replaced by a Supreme Being "who saw neither the suffering of the children in exile nor the injustices of human societies, and who certainly did not intervene in behalf of the poor and the oppressed."[18] González goes further in pointing out the continuing and powerful influence of this idolatrous image of God, especially among professing Christians in the Western world:

> The "God" who passes for the biblical God is used to protect the interests of North American investments overseas. That is the reason why so many people are incensed when they hear that Christians in the Third World are opposed to such interests, which to them is like opposing God. The idol, joined with the military-industrial-academic complex, supports the building of bigger and more devastating bombs, all in the name of the survival of Western civilization, which has come to be equated with Christianity.[19]

The Crucified God

In the aftermath of the Second World War, with cities across Europe, both East and West, in ruins, and with the horrific images of the Holocaust seared into the consciousness of existing and future generations, Christianity confronted a crisis of faith which had close parallels with that experienced centuries earlier by the Jewish people in the time of the prophet Jeremiah. Indeed, a modern Jewish writer commented that no theologian "could speak effectively to his time during the first half of the twentieth century" unless he were deeply cognizant "of the universal dissolution in two world wars of the old certainties of European civilization."[20] The writer had himself studied under Paul Tillich, a survivor of the First World War who as a young chaplain in the German army had witnessed some of the most terrible battles of that conflict and was later to speak of the "shaking of the foundations" of the Western world.[21]

---

18. González, *Mañana*, 98.

19. González, 100.

20. Richard L. Rubenstein, *After Auschwitz: Radical Theology and Contemporary Judaism* (New York: Bobbs-Merrill, 1966), 206–207.

21. In a volume of his university sermons published in 1949 Tillich said that whenever man claimed to be like God, "he has been rebuked and brought to self-destruction and despair." This he saw as the root cause of the collapse of the foundations of Western civilization and he spoke of seeing "American soldiers walking through the ruins of [European] cities, thinking of their own country, and seeing with visionary clarity the doom of its towns and cities." These soldiers were given a prophetic insight "not very different from the message of the Hebrew prophets." Paul Tillich, *The Shaking of the Foundations* (Harmondsworth: Penguin, 1949), 16–17.

Alan Lewis has observed that the "sheer force" of historical experience in the twentieth century

> helped to push theology toward the thinking of new thoughts about a suffering, crucified, buried God. After two World Wars and many "lesser" conflicts, the Holocaust and other genocides, the new palpability of worldwide hunger, poverty and violence conveyed by modern media, and the measurable dying of the planet itself, the stench of death hangs over us all today as perhaps no previous generation.[22]

Lewis's remarkable book explores in great detail the reality of the challenges to faith in what we have earlier described as an "Easter Saturday" culture, a context within which the names of Auschwitz, Hiroshima and Chernobyl represent an epochal change resulting in a new awareness of the pervasive nature and profound depth of human suffering and of the vulnerability of our beautiful planet and all life upon it. Such knowledge cannot be supressed or ignored by those who would "speak of faith and hope and give to love a divine dimension and foundation." At such a time, when we have become "sensitized to the misery endured in gulags and ghettos, prison cells and cancer wards," witness to the gospel can only be credible if it is underpinned by a theology which recognizes "the cross and tomb of Jesus as the loci of *divine suffering and death*" and the revelation of "*the pain and passion of his heavenly Father.* How can we do otherwise than speak to our suffering world of a suffering God?"[23]

Earlier we made reference to Dietrich Bonhoeffer's famous statement, written in a letter in which he confessed that he was "thinking aloud in order to clarify my thoughts," that God had allowed himself "to be edged out of the world and onto the cross." Awaiting imminent execution in his lonely prison cell, Bonhoeffer wrote that instead of encouraging us to look for the intervention of a supremely *powerful* deity, the gospel directs us to the powerlessness of God, so that "it is not by his omnipotence that Christ helps us, but by his weakness and suffering." The crisis of Christendom, perceived with unparalleled clarity by a theologian facing death for his active resistance to Hitler and his repudiation

---

22. Lewis, *Between Cross and Resurrection*, 164.

23. Lewis, 164; emphasis added. Note also the comment of Richard Bauckham: "In Romans 8:32 Paul looks, as it were, upon the crucified Jesus dying in abandonment by God, not from our perspective, but from God the Father's perspective. God, he says, 'did not spare his own Son, but gave him up for us all.' There is real pain in those words." Bauckham goes on to say, "God does not suffer out of weakness as we do. He suffers out of the fullness of his love for us. He suffers the suffering entailed by the relationship of love into which he has voluntarily opted by creating and relating to his creation." *Bible in the Contemporary World*, 136.

of the "cheap grace" which had led the German churches into apostasy, was recognized as a context within which Christians were granted an opportunity to abandon a false conception of God and discover "the God of the Bible, who conquers power and space in the world by his weakness."[24]

Even as Bonhoeffer wrote these lines, his compatriot Jürgen Moltmann was wrestling with precisely the same issues while a prisoner of war behind barbed wire. He later described the impact of the wartime experience on his subsequent life and work: "Shattered and broken, the survivors of my generation were then returning from camps and hospitals to the lecture room. A theology which did not speak of God in the sight of the one who was abandoned and crucified would have nothing to say to us then."[25] In the decades following the Second World War Moltmann was to publish a series of studies which have had a major role in reorienting Christian theology by placing the cross of Jesus Christ at the foundation and heart of the knowledge of God. The real crisis of Christianity in the twentieth century was not, he said, a choice between assimilation to the culture shaped by modernity or a retreat to a religious ghetto in which a conservative form of faith might be preserved, but rather it consisted in "the crisis of its own existence as the church of the crucified Christ." The future of Western Christianity in the post-war world would be determined, Moltmann said, by "whether the crucified Christ is a stranger to it or the Lord who determines the form of its existence."

I first encountered Moltmann's work when, during a summer break in my studies at the University of Aberdeen in the 1980s, I returned to Nigeria to teach a course in the Samuel Bill Theological College. As I shared earlier in this book, this was a period of intense personal struggle for me as I wrestled with questions arising from my previous experience of life on the African continent and with the challenges to faith then emerging from my academic studies of secularization. In this context, reading Moltmann's *The Crucified God* (often

---

24. Bonhoeffer, *Letters and Papers from Prison*, 122; emphasis added.

25. Jürgen Moltmann, *The Crucified God: The Cross of Christ as the Foundation and Criticism of Christian Theology* (London: SCM, 1974), 1. Moltmann elsewhere describes himself as belonging "to the generation which consciously lived through the horrors of the Second World War, the collapse of an empire and all its institutions, the guilt and shame of one's own nation, and a long period as a prisoner of war." Weighed down by "the sombre burden of a guilt that could never be paid off," his generation felt "an inconsolable grief." He testifies to an experience of God in the dark night of the soul: "What I felt all at once was the death of all the mainstays that had sustained my life up to then. It was only slowly that something different began to build up in their stead. . . . And yet the experience of misery and forsakenness and daily humiliation gradually built up into an experience of God." Behind barbed wire he found "a hope which wants something new, instead of seeking a return to the old." *Experiences of God* (Philadelphia: Fortress, 1980), 6–8.

by the light of a bush lamp when the generator had failed or been switched off)
was a revelation to me since the book seemed to respond directly to many of the
issues with which I was wrestling. Moltmann engaged with the writers whose
work I had been reading during my studies, including Albert Camus whose
deeply honest objections to faith had so impressed me. Moltmann described
the rejection of religion by such contemporary thinkers as "protest atheism,"
since their difficulties were not related to philosophy, nor to the challenge
posed by science, but precisely to *suffering* – especially, in the case of Camus,
the suffering of *children*. The only possibility of a credible response to such
objections to belief in God, Moltmann said, was "through a theology of the
cross which understands God in the suffering of Christ and which cries out
with the godforsaken God, 'My God, why have you forsaken me?'"[26]

> For this theology, God and suffering are no longer contradictions,
> as in theism and atheism, but God's being is in suffering and the
> suffering is in God's being itself, because God is love. . . . He is no
> "cold heavenly power" nor does he "tread his way over corpses,"
> but is known as the human God in the crucified Son of Man.[27]

Moltmann showed how the transformation which takes place in our
understanding of the being of God when the death of the cross becomes
the foundation of theology provides the basis for a pastoral response to the
anguished questions arising in contexts of great loss and suffering. God in
Christ "enters into the limited, finite situation of man" and "accepts and
embraces the whole of human existence with his being." God's action in the
incarnation and cruel death of his Son is the divine response to all the cries
of lament in a fallen and broken world, so that there "is no loneliness and no
rejection which [God] has not taken to himself and assumed in the cross of
Jesus."[28]

However, Moltmann's theology of the cross moves beyond the concerns of
pastoral care within the believing community to provide a basis, an imperative,
for Christian social and political engagement in the broken world. The crux
of my personal struggle when returning to the Western world had been the
urgent quest for a bridge between what I believed as a Christian and a praxis

---

26. Moltmann, *Crucified God*, 227.

27. Moltmann, 227.

28. Moltmann, 277. Note the comment of Richard Bauckham and Trevor Hart: "The cross
where Jesus drank to the dregs the cup of God-forsaken death, is not a stage in the upward
ascent of human history, but a descent into its depths in order to bring God into those depths."
Hope against Hope: Christian Eschatology in Contemporary Context (London: Darton, Longman
& Todd, 1999), 40.

which I now saw to be demanded as the result of knowledge of the extent of the suffering of so many fellow human beings. In addition, I felt a deepening conviction that their plight was related to the injustices and inequalities which were embedded within the social, economic and political systems shaping the modern world. Imagine, then, my reaction to the discovery of Moltmann's insistence that many historical traditions of interpretation of the cross, together with long-established patterns of devotion in worship and hymnology, *subverted* the true significance of Calvary, evading the *scandal* of this event and concealing both its horror and revolutionary implications.

> The symbol of the cross in the church points to the God who was crucified not between two candles on an altar, but between two thieves in the place of the skull, where the outcasts belong, outside the gates of the city. . . . It is a symbol which therefore leads out of the church and out of religious longing into the fellowship of the oppressed and abandoned. On the other hand, it is a symbol which calls the oppressed and godless into the church and through the church into the fellowship of the crucified God.[29]

Speaking of God in a Globalized World

I referred above to the emergence of "a global chorus singing new songs." The second half of the twentieth century revealed both the extent and the depth of the crisis facing Christianity in its former European heartlands, while at the same time evidence accumulated of its phenomenal growth across the southern hemisphere. We have by now become familiar with the reality of a "shift in the centre of gravity" of the Christian faith on a global scale, a phrase which signifies a social and cultural transformation which is likely

---

29. Moltmann, 40. Moltmann's theology of the cross stands within a tradition which can be traced back to Martin Luther and his distinction between a "theology of glory" and a "theology of the cross." It also builds on the work of Karl Barth who, in Alan Lewis's words, had earlier "learned dramatically to rethink the very doctrine of God in the light of Jesus' death and burial. Here the already tottering edifice of immutability collapsed, terminally shaken by the revealed actuality of God's Christomorphic passion." Lewis, *Between Cross and Resurrection*, 197. We should also note the extraordinary work of G. K. Chesterton who, in a book with the title *Orthodoxy* (1908), wrote: "And now let all the revolutionists choose a creed from all the creeds and a god from all the gods of the world, carefully weighing all the gods of inevitable recurrence and unalterable power. They will not find another god who has himself been in revolt. Nay (the matter grows too difficult for human speech) but let the atheists themselves choose a god. They will find only one divinity who uttered their isolation: only one religion in which God seemed for an instant to be an atheist." G. K. Chesterton, *Orthodoxy*, Project Gutenberg eBook, accessed 2 October 2018, www.gutenberg.org/cache/epub/130/pg130-images.html.

to prove even more significant than that which occurred when the gospel took root in the soil of the Hellenistic culture of the ancient world. This time the transformation of Christianity is not the result of the crossing of a single cultural barrier, but is the outcome of multiple processes of translation through which Christ is now confessed as Lord in a huge range of cultural and linguistic contexts. It is a striking fact, frequently overlooked in Western discussions of the contemporary state of the world, that at the very point at which globalization has extended the reach of Western models of development and capitalism to every part of the world, Christianity has become a *non-Western religion.* This still-occurring transformation involves a fundamental shift in the social and cultural identity of the Christian movement since the new heartlands reflect not only a geographical shift from north to south, but also a downward social movement resulting in the religion having its greatest strength in the margins of a globalized world. The message of the crucified God has been received with gladness among millions of uprooted and displaced people, including slum-dwellers whose numbers grow exponentially in what has been called the "endless city." To put this bluntly, world Christianity in the early twenty-first century is no longer a privileged white man's religion, but has returned to a place similar to its original social location at the margins of political and economic power, a shift which holds the promise of an historically unprecedented opportunity to rediscover the core message of the cross and of the hope made possible by the resurrection.

The emergence of world Christianity has, among many other significant changes, resulted in the renewed prominence in worship and prayer of the *biblical lament.* There are many reasons for this; the new geographical locations of Christianity are often in regions of the world, especially in Asia, where cataclysmic disasters resulting from earthquakes, typhoons, tsunamis and floods are part of "normal life" and compel the asking of honest questions concerning divine providence. To confess faith while living in the frozen wastes of the polar extremes, or amid the heat and humidity of the tropics, is to face challenges arising from natural environments which are unknown to Christians in more temperate climates. Again, whereas until modern times European Christians never encountered people belonging to other faith traditions, the new heartlands of the Jesus movement are invariably characterized by religious pluralism, so that the confession of Christ is made in cultural contexts profoundly shaped by other ancient religious traditions. This may result in suffering or persecution, but even where this is not the case Christians have to wrestle with difficult issues concerning their identity which never faced believers within the boundaries of European Christendom. Above all, however, world Christianity in a globalized era confronts the challenges of systemic injustice and oppression which result in endemic poverty, hunger and death, so that entire populations in many parts of the Majority World have been described as "crucified peoples." In these situations the spirituality of lament becomes absolutely critical to the survival of faith and its credibility in situations where millions of people exist at the edge of life and death.

From the very dawn of the modern age and the beginning of the global expansion of Western political and economic power, aboriginal people on every continent on earth have experienced revolutionary changes which threatened their traditional ways of life and undermined both social cohesion and material well-being.[30] Perhaps the most tragic example of such suffering concerns the slave trade which devastated large parts of Africa, created a terrible legacy which is still being played out in the Americas, and casts a long, dark shadow across Europe, where questions concerning the human cost of the development of many celebrated urban centres continue to be suppressed.

The experience of slavery brought with it multiple causes of human trauma and, for a deeply religious African people, a sense of utter godforsakenness. The response of many African slaves in this context was extraordinary in that they articulated their agony and despair in the shape of new forms of lament with close parallels to those found on the pages of the Bible. We refer, of course, to the African-American spiritual songs which over time have come to exercise a profound influence on Western consciousness and culture.[31] These songs confirm what we have noticed earlier in this book, that music and poetry play key roles in the human response to trauma and extreme suffering, and while African-American spiritual songs constitute a completely original form of expression, "they are no less significant as a source of theology for the people who birthed them than Jewish psalms are for the people who brought them forth."[32]

---

30. See Mark Cocker, *Rivers of Blood, Rivers of Gold: Europe's Conflict with Tribal Peoples* (London: Pimlico, 1999). We discuss the African experience below but Cocker surveys the impact of European expansion across the globe, including the loss of eleven million lives among indigenous peoples in Mexico following the Spanish invasion, the decimation of aboriginal populations in Brazil following the Portuguese conquest, and the tragic history of native North American peoples. Some historians have put the total loss of human lives in the Americas resulting from the expansion of the West as high as one hundred million people.

31. When the English composer Michael Tippett, who was himself imprisoned as a pacifist during the Second World War, came to write a post-war oratorio telling the story of a young Jewish boy executed by the Nazis in Paris, he incorporated four African-American spirituals in the composition, including "Nobody Knows the Trouble I See" and "Deep River."

32. David Emmanuel Goatley, *Were You There? Godforsakenness in Slave Religion* (Maryknoll, NY: Orbis, 1996), 45.

Studies of the theology expressed in African-American spirituals conclude that they return again and again to the crucifixion and discover a parallel between the horror of Calvary and the physical, emotional and spiritual agonies of slave life. The songs express a conviction that Jesus "identified with slaves in a particular way" and that in their turn, they possessed a unique perspective on his suffering.[33]

> Were you there when they crucified my Lord?
> Oh! Sometimes it causes me to tremble, tremble, tremble.

This has been described as "one of the great poems of all time," not least because its repeated questioning suggests that every great wrong, all the crimes against humanity, are "committed under the eyes of frightened or uncaring people." The finger of accusation points to us all: we "are guilty not so much because of what we do, as what we allow to happen. And without a doubt, the slave singer was including slavery of human flesh in the bill of indictment."[34]

If lament resurfaced to play a central role in the response to the suffering of slaves, it has reappeared throughout sub-Saharan Africa itself in more recent times in a situation in which an entire continent suffers beneath the burden of the colonial legacy and the failure of independent African governments to fulfil their promises of liberation and freedom. In the early years of the present century I visited Nairobi on a number of occasions, spending time with Christian brothers and sisters in Kibera, widely regarded as Africa's largest slum. On one occasion, coming away from Kibera with a heavy heart and a troubled conscience, I stumbled on a bookshop in which I found a copy of Jean-Marc Ela's *African Cry*. The title itself speaks the language of lament, and that night as I devoured Ela's pages I realized that I had found an African Christian theologian whose work responded to the nest of issues which burned within my soul. Ela was a Cameroonian Catholic who had completed a doctorate in theology in Paris and later returned to France to work for a second doctorate in sociology. With an educational achievement which would have opened almost any career doors for him in post-colonial Africa, this remarkable man chose to devote his life to the service of a neglected and suffering tribal people in the remote mountains of northern Cameroon. He wrote that the birthplace of his published theological reflections was "the villages of the lowlands and the

---

33. Richard Cassidy discusses the significance of the Johannine narrative in which Jesus washes the feet of his "slaves," elevating them to the status of "friends" (John 13:4–6). He concludes: "Seemingly John anticipates an end to the purchasing of slaves by Christians. For are not all purchased slaves potentially Christians? And, as Christians, are they not subjects (not objects) whose feet are to be washed by their masters?" *John's Gospel in New Perspective*, 122.

34. John Lovell Jr., *Black Song: The Forge and the Flame* (New York: Macmillan, 1972), 304.

mountains where we went on foot, our only baggage a sleeping mat, a Bible, our heart, and the love of the poor."[35]

Out of this truly apostolic mission there emerged a series of reflections on Christianity in Africa which, to my knowledge, are unrivalled in their insight, passion and prophetic courage. I have written elsewhere on the significance of Ela's work,[36] but here we note an example of his writing which has a direct bearing on the subject of this chapter. He is discussing "an African reading of the Exodus":

> The God of the Old Testament, the God of Promise, continually shows human beings a future of hope, which enables them to criticize the existing situation. God summons up from within the hoping consciousness of the human being a nonconformity with reality. In short, God carries human beings forward, toward a future characterized by a new reality. But in the official churches, God's divinity has been posited in a changelessness, an immutability, an impassibility such that the history of human beings is effectively abandoned to its own devices, deprived of the capacity to appear as the locus of manifestation of God's action. If the God of preaching . . . is simply the God of Greek metaphysics, then God is nothing but a supreme, eternal idea, having no connection with anything that happens on earth, where human beings live their lives.[37]

Ela was fiercely critical of a Catholicism which confined faith within "a religious world limited to the sacraments and grace" at a time when the agents of foreign economic and financial power argued over African "land, beaches, bauxite, copper and diamond mines, commerce and tourism, and of course uranium and petrol." While the phenomenal growth of Christianity in sub-Saharan Africa was an undeniable reality, its potentially transformative impact was being neutered by the privatization of faith, allowing free reign to those forces which were turning the continent into "a sort of fiscal paradise for multinationals which demand a climate of stability and security as a precondition for the organised pillage of national resources."[38] As will be

---

35. Jean-Marc Ela, *My Faith as an African* (Nairobi: Acton, 2001), xix.

36. David Smith, "Theology as a Voice for the Voiceless: Jean-Marc Ela's *African Cry*," *Theological College of Northern Nigeria Research Bulletin* 52 (March 2010): 19–29.

37. Jean-Marc Ela, *African Cry* (Eugene, OR: Wipf & Stock, 2005), 30.

38. Jean-Marc Ela, *From Charity to Liberation* (London: Catholic Institute for International Relations, 1984), 12–13.

obvious, Ela combined deep learning and a powerful critical intelligence with a sincere love for the poor and oppressed, and he displayed remarkable courage and a willingness to suffer as the result of the inevitable reaction to his outspokenness from both his church and political rulers in his native Cameroon. His voice is one which still needs to be heard, primarily across post-colonial Africa, but in the contemporary West as well. His time in France had shown him that talk of God in Europe was "socially insignificant" and that atheism seemed to have become "a social necessity." He asked penetrating questions: "What God do the people in the West believe in? What is the good news for those who live in dominating societies?" His reply resonates long after his death in 2008:

> In the painful march of the peoples of the Third World toward the victory of life, perhaps Christians should remember that the God of Life has lifted up the poor and fed the hungry. Today that God calls us to struggle for justice and right. Then we shall be able to sing the Magnificat, not in Latin, but in deeds, wherever faith is lived among the poor. We shall be able to sing the Magnificat in the slums, in the villages, in the streets – wherever we are – because the truth of God is fully engaged both in the countries of hunger and in the dominating societies.[39]

It would not be an exaggeration to say that the "march of the peoples of the Third World toward the victory of life" appears to have stalled in the decade since Ela's passing. In particular on the continent of Africa the aftermath of the Rwandan genocide was marked by terrible violence spilling across the borders of neighbouring countries and engulfing the entire region in seemingly endless conflict. Scholars have struggled to grasp the causes and intractable nature of these conflicts, yet they use phrases like Africa's *world war* to highlight the seriousness and global significance of the still-unfolding tragedies and to suggest that the scale of this catastrophe can be likened to that which devastated Europe in the last century.[40]

For a contemporary African theologian like Emmanuel Katangole, the tragedy occurring across the whole of central Africa compels the asking of

---

39. Ela, *My Faith as an African*, 100.

40. The starting point in any attempt to understand these events must be Adam Hochschild's *King Leopold's Ghost: A Story of Greed, Terror and Heroism in Colonial Africa* (London: Pan, 2012). Recent studies include Jason K. Stearns, *Dancing in the Glory of Monsters: The Collapse of the Congo and the Great War of Africa* (New York: Public Affairs, 2011) and Gerard Prunier, *Africa's World War: The Congo, the Rwandan Genocide, and the Making of a Continental Catastrophe* (Oxford: Oxford University Press, 2011).

painful questions concerning the social, cultural and political influence of Christianity. As we have noted above, the *growth* of churches throughout sub-Saharan Africa has been phenomenal, yet this very fact demands that we confront critical questions concerning the relationship between the profession of faith and the collapse of the very foundations of social life in country after country in different parts of the continent. Katangole describes how, having witnessed the rise of the "Lord's Resistance Army" in his native Uganda, resulting in the maiming and deaths of huge numbers of people, the terrorizing of an entire population, the tragic abduction of over 26,000 children, and then the unspeakable horrors of the Rwanda holocaust and the seemingly never-ending sufferings of the peoples of the Congo, he "began to wonder about the difference that Christianity makes – or can make – in Africa."[41]

> The genocide in Rwanda . . . shattered any naiveté I had about the church and Christianity in Africa. For the Rwanda genocide not only happened in one of the most Christianized nations in Africa; the churches themselves often became killing fields, with Christians killing fellow Christians in the same places they had worshipped together. . . . I kept wondering whether Christianity in Africa had become so interwoven with the story of violence that it no longer had a vantage point from which to resist the violence.[42]

This question is not unique to Africa and African Christianity; for European believers it must trigger recollection of the fact that precisely the same kinds of issues arose on their continent throughout the post-war period of the last century. How could theology be possible after Auschwitz? What had happened in the land of Martin Luther to create a context in which professing Christians remained silent in the face of the rise of fascism and a racialist ideology? At the time of this writing, the surge of what is called "populism," accompanied by the resurfacing of the sort of nationalist rhetoric last heard in Europe in the 1930s, and the apparent indifference of many professing Christians to this sobering reality, makes it clear that we are not dealing here with merely *local* situations. Were that the case we might be able to treat such events as departures from the norm, aberrations which leave a tradition of faithfulness, courage and resistance to evil untarnished. However, the apparent vulnerability of Christianity to movements deploying extreme violence in racist and nationalist causes across time and in diverse historical and political contexts compels us to

---

41. Emmanuel Katangole, *The Sacrifice of Africa: A Political Theology for Africa* (Grand Rapids, MI: Eerdmans, 2011), 7.

42. Katangole, *Sacrifice of Africa*, 8–9.

face the troubling possibility that there is some fundamental weakness within the religion itself. Brian Stanley, in a "World History" of Christianity in the last century, reaches the following conclusion when discussing the genocides of Europe and Africa:

> For Christians, what is doubly disturbing about the unprecedented scale and rate of ethnic killing in these two cases is *the seeming impotence of their faith to resist the destructive power of racial hatred.* The two holocausts – in Nazi Germany and Rwanda . . . tell a depressing story of widespread, though never total, capitulation by churches and Christian leaders to the insidious attractions of racial ideology, and of the habitual silence or inaction of many Christians in the face of observed atrocities.[43]

Here we come full circle because in precisely the tragic situations we have alluded to above, Katangole – consciously following Jean-Marc Ela and others – discovers in the cry of *lament* a response to the disasters destroying the foundations of social life in many parts of Africa. In a book with the significant title *Born from Lament*, he records an extraordinary outburst of poetic and artistic laments in precisely those places where suffering has been most extensive and shows that in the very act of verbalizing the traumas resulting from extreme violence and inhumanity, a means of survival and – even more extraordinarily – of the rebirth of hope appears. Katangole records many of these remarkable poems and concludes that they represent "a profound theological mystery in the same way as the book of Lamentations does: namely, what we encounter in lament is not simply a silent God but a suffering and vulnerable God."[44]

The work of theologians like Ela and Katangole is of absolutely crucial importance for the future of Christianity in Africa, but I suggest that it has a far wider, international resonance in the era of globalization and of world Christianity. In particular, we are compelled to ask, why did songs and prayers of lament disappear from the churches of Europe and North America, and from those non-Western churches in which, as a consequence of Western missionary work, Christianity continues to take imported forms? How could

---

43. Brian Stanley, *Christianity in the Twentieth Century: A World History* (Princeton, NJ: Princeton University Press, 2018), 153–154; emphasis added.

44. Emmanuel Katangole, *Born from Lament: The Theology and Politics of Hope in Africa* (Grand Rapids, MI: Eerdmans, 2017), 100. In addition to the two books already cited, note as well Katangole's *The Journey of Reconciliation: Groaning for a New Creation in Africa* (Maryknoll, NY: Orbis, 2017) and, with Chris Rice, *Reconciling All Things: A Christian Vision of Justice, Peace and Healing* (Downers Grove, IL: InterVarsity Press, 2008).

it have come about that the dialectical pattern of lament and praise, which we have seen to be embedded within the very structure of biblical faith, went missing in Christendom? And is this distortion of Christianity, so that it becomes unremittingly affirmative, positive and celebratory, a significant contributory element to its vulnerability to alien ideologies and movements?

As we have seen in this chapter, a fundamental response to these critically important questions is *theological* in that the absence of lament reflects a particular understanding of the being of God. Walter Brueggemann suggests that when "faith permits and requires this form of prayer," the power dynamics between the intercessor and God are rebalanced, "so that the petitionary party is taken seriously and the God who is addressed is newly engaged in the crisis in a way that puts God at risk."[45] The composer of the lament is recognized and listened to "and God is made available to the petitioner." This is clearly not the case where the only acceptable mode of worship and devotion is praise and the response to suffering, or to the encounter with the dark forces of evil, must always be one of reverent submission to the divine will. The loss or suppression of lament thus creates a spiritual monoculture in which nothing remotely surprising, discouraging or challenging can happen and a "theological monopoly is reinforced."

However, the loss of lament has significance beyond the spiritual and theological realms since when oppressed and suffering peoples articulate their distress in poetry and song, the earthly powers who benefit from the existing structures of political and economic power become extremely nervous. Where lament falls silent, drowned out by the noise of celebration, those who walk through the valley of the shadow of death must hold their tongues and join in praise which they know to be inauthentic.[46] At the same time, the powers that be can rest assured that religion can be viewed as an ally since it appears to be incapable of voicing opposition to injustice and oppression. In Brueggemann's words, "A community of faith that negates laments soon concludes that the hard issues of justice are improper questions to pose at the throne, because the throne seems to be only a place of praise."[47]

---

45. Walter Brueggemann, "The Costly Loss of Lament," in *The Psalms: The Life of Faith*, ed. Patrick D. Miller (Minneapolis: Fortress, 1995), 101.

46. The reference to the "valley of the shadow of death" comes from Psalm 23 and is accompanied by the testimony "I will fear no evil, for you are with me." This confession of the reality of God's presence and faithfulness is, of course, part of the core tradition of the Bible. Yet Psalm 23 is immediately preceded by the lament of Psalm 22: "My God, my God, why have you forsaken me? Why are you so far from saving me, so far from the words of my groaning?"

47. Brueggemann, "Costly Loss of Lament," 107.

Finally, the loss of lament is not unrelated to the culture of *modernity* and the myths of historical progress through the onward march of science and technology which underlie this ideology. A culture which claims to be secular, in which "God" has dropped out of the indexes of every significant discussion of politics, economics and even morality, continues to trumpet its claim to be the only route to human happiness and security. Despite mounting evidence to the contrary in the shape of negative indicators across a whole range of categories of personal and social well-being, we hear voices making ever more strident and hubristic claims for the advent of a utopia in which technology will "defeat death and grant human beings eternal youth."[48] Clearly, lament would become impossible in a world where such a worldview became universal and, in as far as Christians abandon a critical role and become passive consumers of the cornucopia that continues to churn out the products of what has been called "the goods life," the prayer of lament will have no place in worship or discipleship.[49]

Lament, Hope and the Endless City

I have referred a number of times to the work of Alan Lewis and his "theology of holy Saturday." Perhaps the most disturbing feature of this book concerns the author's conclusions with regard to the future of humankind and the planet on which we live. Lewis asks how the reality of the weakness of God revealed at the cross is related to Christian hope and his conclusion, repeated several times and at some length, is that the God of Jesus Christ

> does not and will not prevent the worst denouements of human, global, or cosmic history. The grace which abounds only *after* sin's increase is not by any means impregnable against the disaster in which that sin expands to the magnitude of an Easter Saturday, of an Auschwitz or Hiroshima, of a Third World War or a planetary

---

48. Harari, *Homo Deus*, 27. We have earlier quoted Harari sounding like Nietzsche on steroids, but elsewhere he acknowledges that the "immortals" who will people this planet, and presumably other worlds, in the future will be a privileged elite. For the rest of us, made redundant in millions by a new technological revolution, there will need to be a "new opium of the masses" in the shape of computer games! "Economically redundant people might spend increasing amounts of time within 3D virtual reality worlds, which would provide them with far more excitement and emotional engagement than the 'real world.'" Harari, "The New Opium of the Masses," *The Guardian*, 8 May 2017, 10–11.

49. The phrase "the goods life" comes from Brad S. Gregory, *The Unintended Reformation: How a Religious Revolution Secularized Society* (Cambridge, MA: Belknap Press of Harvard University, 2012). Chapter 5 is entitled "Manufacturing the Goods Life" and is directly relevant to this discussion (235–297).

cataclysm. The Christian story concludes with the pardoning of guilt and the banishing of death, with the redemption of time beyond its rupture and the proleptic dawning of a universal future over the ovens, missile silos, and melting power plants of humanity's hopelessness. Yet the hope which is assured that beyond our atrocities and calamities the God of the cross shall still prevail by the flourishing of risky, vulnerable grace cannot and does not exclude, but must allow space for, the most disproportionate and conclusive of historical disasters.[50]

What this means is spelled out with chilling clarity: after the ghastly experiences of the twentieth century, Christian hope is grounded "in the harsh and harrowing knowledge that the only love able to triumph over those excrescences of wickedness and folly is the love which bows to their occurrence and makes itself their victim."[51] There could scarcely be a more striking contrast in mood than that between this sobering language and the boundless optimism of Christians attending the World Missionary Conference in Edinburgh just over a century ago, their confidence encapsulated in the famous phrase, "Evangelise the world in this generation." However, if that optimism was shown by subsequent history to be misplaced and unfounded, we have to ask whether Lewis's pessimism must also be challenged, not because the threats he describes are exaggerated (they are not), but because the Christian hope found on the pages of Scripture can be read in a different way from this. While Lewis has helped us to recognize the theological significance of the Saturday which intervenes between cross and resurrection, thus providing a necessary corrective to a triumphalist proclamation of the Easter message, that day must not become the primary focus of faith in a manner which would eclipse the good news of the "incomparably great power" with which God overcame death, raising Christ to "his right hand in the heavenly realms, far

---

50. Lewis, *Between Cross and Resurrection*, 298. Earlier he has described this conclusion as the "benumbing possibility" that "the ultimate tomorrow when God shall at last be all in all could follow, not avert, that infinitude of Hiroshimas which would be the holocaust of all humanity" (282). Anyone tempted to doubt the possibility of the "planetary catastrophe" to which Lewis refers should watch the film series *Chernobyl* which reveals just how close we have already been to just such a disaster. ACORN DVD AV3546. Paul Tillich said something similar when he described God as speaking today through the mouths of our greatest scientists: "You yourselves can bring about the end of yourselves. I give the power to shake the foundations of your earth into your hands. You can use this power for creation or destruction. How will you use it?" *Shaking of the Foundations*, 14.

51. Lewis, *Between Cross and Resurrection*, 298.

above all rule and authority, power and dominion," a triumph which is *"for us who believe"* (Eph 1:18–23).[52]

This is not the place to develop an extended discussion of Christian hope, but it is important to state that the weakness of God on which we have reflected in this chapter does not imply a passive helplessness in the face of human rebellion and arrogance, and even less should it be interpreted as a surrender to the powers of darkness. There is no reneging on the promise of *shalom* made to the patriarchs and announced as breaking into history with the coming of Christ. The hope that the purposes of God *within human history* are yet to find a greater outworking in the salvation of "all Israel" and a consequent blessing extending to all peoples is central to Paul's eschatology in Romans 9–11. What makes this passage so significant in relation to our context today is that Paul's extraordinary hope emerges from the crushing disappointment occasioned by the *rejection* of his message by his own people! We have previously noticed the pathos-filled language with which he *laments* the failure of "those of my own race" to embrace Christ (Rom 9:1–3). The words contain clear echoes of the psalms of lament and his experience is analogous to that of the Hebrew prophets. His anguish stems from the depth of his love for his own people and the tragedy of their resistance to the message of the cross, a turn of events which seemed to reverse their anticipated role in the eschatological drama. This situation, which became yet more serious with the subsequent failure of his delivery of "the collection" in Jerusalem, called into question both the power of the gospel and the faithfulness of God with respect to the promises made to Abraham and his descendants. Yet the pain and despair occasioned by these events were assuaged by a fresh revelation of the mystery of the divine purpose through which the very stumbling of Israel became the means of blessing for the nations and the Gentiles' incorporation within the family of God which, in its turn, would ultimately result in Jewish unbelief being overcome. Hope thus emerged out of despair and the "patience" and "kindness" of God were vindicated, even as his judgements were recognized as being "unsearchable" and his "paths beyond tracing out" (11:33). Robert Jewett summarizes the apostle's argument in these chapters as follows:

---

52. Compare the statements of Lewis with these words of Jürgen Moltmann: "Anyone who believes that the world is going to end in a catastrophe will not make a new beginning because it is pointless. Anyone who sees no future before him goes on as before, until he falls backwards into the pit he is digging for himself. For a new beginning we need the power of a hope that transforms life and overcomes the world. . . . The living source of this hope lies in a future from which new time, new potentiality and new freedom continually advance to meet us. We find this future in Jesus Christ; he is our future – he is our hope." *Experiences of God*, 28.

Paul believed that when all the people of the earth accept the gospel, they will all for the first time praise God rather than themselves. The competition between nations that had always brought war and destruction will thereby come to an end. The Pauline hope of a world-transforming mission is viewed as a fulfilment of biblical prophecy, that all nations will find in the Messiah a new and peaceful destiny, including solidarity with one another. To whittle back the details of Paul's vision to more "reasonable" levels, reflecting the fact of their nonfulfillment in the twenty centuries past, undercuts the magnificent scope of the "mystery" that Paul believed he had been given.[53]

Thus, Paul can celebrate the weakness of God because the life and death of Jesus and the Pentecostal gift of the Holy Spirit display the transformative and reconciling power of divine love, so that God's weakness "is *stronger than man's strength*" (1 Cor 1:25). So important is this principle that elsewhere he applies it to his own experience and says that he *delights* in weakness since, in a paradox that is fundamental to his life and ministry, he testifies that "*when I am weak, then I am strong*" (2 Cor 12:8–10). In other words, through the incarnation a form of radical love has been released into this broken world which challenges and subverts existing structures of power, exposes the hidden, camouflaged motives which lie behind them, and demolishes the fabricated justifications used to defend them, while offering humankind a concrete example of a radically different way of being a human family. Ulrich Mauser, whose work we noticed in a previous chapter, points out that the followers of Jesus addressed in the letters to the Colossians and Ephesians remained a small minority of the population in these cities, yet their task was to "image a new vision and reality: that of a global human community no longer torn apart by hostility." The term "global" is anachronistic in regard to the first century but not in the twenty-first when, with the emergence of world Christianity, we may hope for the "growth of the church into a holy temple of the one God" (Eph 2:21) and a consequent process of healing and reconciliation, creating "a new unity in the human race and an expansion of the peace realized in this unity."[54]

The threats which confront humankind and the planet which is its home are as grave and urgent as Alan Lewis has described them and they will be

---

53. Jewett, *Romans: A Commentary*, Hermeneia, 702.

54. Mauser, *Gospel of Peace*, 163. He goes on to say: "The growth of the church is intended to advance the unity and peace of this new community, the signpost and pioneer of an ultimate unity and peace in which all who are members of the global human family are united."

averted only by a counter-cultural movement on a global scale, the like of which has never yet been seen in the course of human history.[55] The crucial question which remains to be faced is whether world Christianity, with its centre of gravity located in the non-Western world, and its experience of suffering, injustice and despair triggering an outpouring of lament and of deep longing for the coming of the reign of God, may yet become the catalyst for just such an uprising against the tragic disorder of the world. Were that to happen, Paul's great vision would cease to be merely a future hope and would enter the realm of historical reality, while God's intention that through Jesus Christ "all things" might be reconciled to himself (Col 1:20) would move nearer to its fulfilment.

---

55. Contemporary thinkers such as Slavoj Žižek warn that we live today "in an apocalyptic time" with grave threats at many levels. He describes how Chinese scientists "have completed the fourth human genome to be sequenced worldwide" and that this research is "the tip of an iceberg of a process going on in China." These developments accelerate the movement toward "the dystopian vision of the state controlling and steering the biogenetic mass of its citizens, but also toward vast profit making: billions of US dollars are invested in labs and clinics (the biggest one in Shanghai) to develop commercial clinics that will target rich Western foreigners who, due to legal prohibitions, will not be able to get this kind of treatment in their own countries." "Thinking Backward: Predestination and Apocalypse," in *Paul's New Moment: Continental Philosophy and the Future of Christian Theology*, ed. John Milbank, Slavoj Žižek and Creston Davis (Grand Rapids, MI: Brazos, 2010), 185–190. It is developments like those described by Žižek which fuel the claims of people like Yuval Harari that we stand at the dawn of a time when humans will become gods. Žižek's response is to recognize the potential of "a radical community of believers . . . along the lines of the original Christian community: a community of outcasts." As a "radical leftist" he thinks "Christianity is far too precious a thing to leave to conservative fundamentalists" (181). Žižek is not a Christian in any sense in which that identity is usually understood, yet the dialogue he and other thinkers have engaged in with theologians like John Milbank and Creston Davis is very significant.

For Reflection

> Oh, the depth of the riches of the
> wisdom and knowledge of God!
> How unsearchable his judgements,
> and his paths beyond tracing out!
> "Who has known the mind of the Lord?
> Or who has been his counsellor?"
> "Who has ever given to God
> that God should repay him?"
> For from him and through him and to him are all things.
> To him be the glory for ever! Amen. (Rom 11:33–36)

It is . . . hard for the mind of man to believe that any member of a species that can organize or even witness the murder of millions and feel no regret should ever be endowed with the ability to receive a thought of God. If man can remain callous to the horror of exterminating millions of men, women and children; if man can be bloodstained and self-righteous, distort what his conscience tells, make soap of human flesh, then how can we assume that he is worthy of being approached and guided by the infinite God?

Man rarely comprehends how dangerously mighty he is. In our own days it is becoming obvious . . . that unless man attaches himself to a source of spiritual power – a match for the energy that he is now able to exploit – a few men may throw all men into final disaster. There is only one source: the will and wisdom of the living God.[56]

---

56. Heschel, *God in Search of Man*, 170–171.

6

Biblical Lament and the Future for World Christianity

In the course of the argument unfolded in the previous chapters there has been a convergence between the pastoral and theological concern with the importance of recovering the biblical tradition of the prayer of lament, on the one hand, and the emergence and growing significance of world Christianity within the context of the global crisis of our times, on the other. As a result, the crucial issue which remains to be faced has become clear: does the shift in the centre of gravity of the *ekklesia* of Christ presage a completely new age in which Christian theology and spirituality will be transformed, deepened and enriched by the experience of members of this body from every continent on earth, and might this result in new ways of being Christian which would contribute toward the substantial healing of our broken world and the triumph of life over the forces of death?

In a footnote at the conclusion of the previous chapter I referred to the work of the philosopher Slavoj Žižek. He has described what he calls "the three main versions of Christianity" as Orthodoxy, Catholicism and Protestantism, each "subdivision" being "split off from a previous unity." Žižek suggests that each of these traditions was shaped by a particular apostolic figure and emerged within a specific historical and cultural context.[1] His discussion may be illustrated by the following diagram, although I have added the suggestion that each tradition may also be associated with a particular *geographical* context.

---

1. Slavoj Žižek and Boris Gunjevic, *God in Pain: Inversions of Apocalypse* (New York: Seven Stories, 2012), 158–160.

Orthodoxy	Catholicism	Protestantism
John	Peter	Paul
Greek/Slavic	Latin	German
Eastern	Western	Northern

Figure 6.1: Major Traditions in the History of Western Christianity

As an aid to the understanding of the history of Western, largely European Christianity this is helpful. However, on a global scale and in the light of the developments we have discussed in the previous chapter, these traditions taken singly, or all of them taken together, are *local* forms of Christianity. Although often regarded by their adherents as expressions of universal truth, they are all in reality partial (one might even say fragmentary) articulations of the fullness of the gospel. We might add that while this model provides us with valuable insight into the history of Christianity across the previous two millennia, it represents the *past* expansion of the movement, its successive permeation of different cultures, regions and peoples, but also its *failure* to retain an overarching unity transcending its legitimate diversity.[2] However – and this is the crucial point – in the globalized world of the twenty-first century, these regional expressions of the Christian movement can no longer claim universal validity, but while sharing their particular insights into the meaning of Christ they must be willing to listen to and learn from the new movements emerging from below. How might we represent this transformation of Christianity in relation to Žižek's schema?

---

2. Even then we must add a significant qualification since, as Philip Jenkins has pointed out, the shape of Christian history with which we are familiar "is a radical departure from what was for well over a millennium the historical norm: another, earlier global Christianity once existed. For most of its history, Christianity was a tri-continental religion, with powerful representation in Europe, Africa and Asia, and this was true into the fourteenth century." *The Lost History of Christianity: The Thousand-Year Golden Age of the Church in the Middle East, Africa and Asia – And How It Died* (New York: HarperOne, 2008), 3.

Orthodoxy	Catholicism	Protestantism	World Christianity
John	Peter	Paul	Jesus
Slavic	Latin	German	Multi-cultural
Eastern	Western	Northern	Southern

Figure 6.2: The Emergence and Significance of World Christianity

The additional column signifies the emergence, not merely of another "subdivision" leading to yet further fragmentation of the Christian movement, but rather of something which can be described as genuinely new. Andrew Walls, who has contributed more to our awareness and understanding of the extent and significance of this phenomenon than almost anyone else, observes that the central issues for Christianity in this new era "will be about how African and Indian and Chinese and Korean and Hispanic and North American and European Christians can together make real the body of Christ." The emergence of distinctively *Southern* forms of the faith means that "the key events in the Christian sphere will increasingly be those taking place in Africa, Asia and Latin America."[3] The significance of this shift in the cultural, social and geographical locations of Christianity is massive, since it involves a move away from the Christendom model which has shaped the traditions of the past, and because the histories, cultures and even climatic and geological contexts of the Majority World pose challenges and questions which have not arisen in Europe or North America. For example, Michael Nai-Chiu Poon observes that the context of the Pacific Rim demonstrates the new foundation for world Christianity since "it opens up spiritual horizons and awakens moral tasks that Christendom experiences cannot reveal." Precisely the fecundity of the new contexts in the Pacific Rim and elsewhere offer a global church the possibility of discovering a "new theological grammar, syntax and semantics for today's world."[4]

---

3. Andrew F. Walls, *The Cross-Cultural Process in Christian History* (Edinburgh: T&T Clark, 2002), 69.

4. Poon, "Rise of Asian Pacific Christianity," 70. Elsewhere he writes that "vulnerability, volatility and fragility are the central features of life in Asia. To the present day, migrant workers, refugees of war and stateless peoples testify to the fluid conditions in human life that are punctuated by the eruptions of wars, tsunamis and earthquakes. Makeshift tents replace cathedrals as the carriers of Christianity at the start of the third millennium. Peoples are on the move; and so too faith is on the move" (69).

Meantime, a second glance at the diagram above suggests that what distinguishes this era from all that has gone before is that the focal point will no longer be determined by secondary figures from the apostolic period, *but is created by Jesus Christ, crucified, buried and risen.* Jaroslav Pelikan closes his wonderful study of the place of Jesus in the history of culture with the statement that "as respect for the organized church has declined, reverence for Jesus has grown," so that he has become "the man who belongs to the world."[5] That "belonging" was already anticipated in the universalism of the New Testament, but only now with the emergence of world Christianity in the era of globalization is it becoming a historical reality, with the result that Western traditions of theology and spirituality long regarded as definitive are shown to be highly contextual, and even somewhat parochial.[6] In a remarkably prescient book published in 1968, Kenneth Cragg concluded:

> As the Christ of Galilee and Jerusalem in New Testament times became the Christ of the Mediterranean, of Athens and Rome, so the Christ of the West must be more evidently the Christ of the world. It is the conviction of Christian faith that He is only known anywhere in His fullness, when the whole world, in its cultural diversity, takes possession of Him and in freedom, in thought and in form, tells of Him what it learns and loves.[7]

Consciousness of this transformation and its implications for the future shape of Christianity and its testimony in a broken world is alive and growing across the southern hemisphere. Consider the representative voices of theologians from the Philippines who comment that times have changed from the era of the dominance of Western models of theology stressing intellectual coherence in the form of doctrines to be believed, to a global context of faith which creates "an increased recognition of a polycentric world and a polycentric world Christianity, with emphasis on many theological centres."

---

5. Jaroslav Pelikan, *Jesus through the Centuries: His Place in the History of Culture* (New York: Harper & Row, 1985), 232.

6. Note the comment of Kevin Vanhoozer: "Christian identity stems from our common effort to speak and do the truth of Jesus Christ in our respective contexts, in full awareness that we are not the only truth seekers, speakers, and sufferers to do so. . . . What is different about doing theology in an era of world Christianity is our awareness of how narrow *our* way of pursuing 'the way' really is." "'One Rule to Rule Them All?' Theological Method in an Era of World Christianity," in *Globalizing Theology: Belief and Practice in the Era of World Christianity*, ed. Craig Ott and Harold Netland (Nottingham: Apollos, 2007), 124.

7. Kenneth Cragg, *Christianity in World Perspective* (London: Lutterworth, 1968), 195.

They conclude that the "future beckons for a truly catholic Christianity that honors unity-in-diversity in both church and theology."[8]

Which brings us to the central issue raised by this present book: *can we hope that a still-emerging world Christianity will grow into a multi-cultural community united in a new form of catholicism and characterized by the practice of a biblical pattern of spirituality in which the interaction between praise and lament sustains the hope of shalom for a still broken and bleeding world?* The previous chapter would suggest that if this is to happen Christians in the West have much to learn from their brothers and sisters across the Majority World, beginning with an understanding of the interrelatedness of our world and the social, cultural and economic consequences of the security and prosperity which they have so long taken for granted.[9]

Weeping with Those Who Weep

Claus Westermann, whose work on the psalms we introduced earlier in this book, comments that the real function of the lament is "to appeal to God's compassion." The lament "implores God to be compassionate to those who suffer," giving voice to human beings in the whole range of afflictions: "oppression, anxiety, pain, and peril are given voice in the lament, and thus it becomes an appeal to the only court that can alter their plight." He reaffirms the

---

8. T. D. Gener and L. Bautista, "Theological Method," in *Global Dictionary of Theology: A Resource for the Worldwide Church*, ed. William Dyrness and Veli-Matti Kärkkäinen (Downers Grove, IL: IVP Academic, 2008), 894. This volume is itself a highly significant indication of the extent of the global transformation now occurring within Christianity. The mention of "catholicity" raises a central theme in much of the reflection now taking place on the emerging shape of the world Christian movement. See especially the contributions of Roman Catholic theologians as follows: Robert Schreiter, *The New Catholicity: Theology between the Global and the Local* (Maryknoll, NY: Orbis, 2004); and William R. Burrows, "Conversion: Individual and Cultural," in *Understanding World Christianity: The Vision and Work of Andrew F. Walls*, ed. William Burrows, Mark Gornik and Janice McLean (Maryknoll, NY: Orbis, 2011), 109–126 (note especially his discussion of catholicity and apostolicity on 123–124).

9. As indicated above, the work of Andrew Walls has been seminal in relation to our understanding of the emergence of world Christianity. In addition to the volume mentioned previously see also his *Missionary Movement in Christian History: Studies in the Transmission of Faith* (Edinburgh: T&T Clark, 1996) and *Crossing Cultural Frontiers: Studies in the History of World Christianity* (Maryknoll, NY: Orbis, 2017). See also Burrows, Gornik and McLean, *Understanding World Christianity*; Wilbert Shenk, ed., *Enlarging the Story: Perspectives on Writing World Christian History* (Maryknoll, NY: Orbis, 2002); Lamin Sanneh, *Whose Religion Is Christianity? The Gospel beyond the West* (Grand Rapids, MI: Eerdmans, 2003); Philip Jenkins, *The Next Christendom: The Coming of Global Christianity* (New York: Oxford University Press, 2002) and *The New Faces of Christianity: Believing the Bible in the Global South* (New York: Oxford University Press, 2006); Lamin Sanneh and Joel Carpenter, eds., *The Changing Face of Christianity: Africa, the West, and the World* (New York: Oxford University Press, 2005).

centrality of lament within the Hebrew Bible, but adds that there is nothing in the New Testament that even hints that "faith in Christ excluded lamentation from a person's relationship with God." Indeed, the depictions of Jesus in the gospels stress over and over again his endless *compassion* for suffering people, whether individuals in distress or the crowds which placed such relentless pressure on his time and energy. The cries for help which echo through the gospels were expressions of lament directed to someone whose love and kindness reflected that of Yahweh and brought healing and deliverance to the oppressed and suffering. "Certainly in the Gospels the actions of Jesus of Nazareth are characterized by the compassion he evidenced for those who implored him to help them in their need. The cry of distress with which the afflicted besought him ('Oh, Thou Son of David, have mercy on me') is never rebuffed by Jesus."[10]

In other words, the life of Jesus reproduces and makes visible on the stage of human history the Hebrew pattern of lament, of cries of distress in a broken world, and the response in the form of divine healing and deliverance, which then triggers outbursts of praise and joy and the creation of a new community. The inexhaustible compassion of Jesus, his patience with the crowds and his tears, both at the encounter with the untimely death of a friend and at the traumas he knew would overwhelm the victims of urbicide in Jerusalem, revealed a love reflecting that of Yahweh in the Hebrew Bible. In his correspondence to Corinth, Paul praises "the God and Father of our Lord Jesus Christ, the *Father of compassion and the God of all comfort*" (2 Cor 1:3). The language appears to suggest that Jesus was *compassion incarnate*, that in him the very nature of God was displayed in a human person whose boundless love for the lost, the lonely and the oppressed resulted in a veritable explosion of joy and thanksgiving. So great was the impact of that life that it became the model for a new, reconciled humankind, a community in which the kindness discovered in Jesus was to be imitated in life together, which then became the magnet which attracted seekers from a world torn apart by tensions, hatred and violence.

If, then, the spirituality and prayers of the first followers of Jesus were shaped by the pattern of praise and lament inherited from the history of biblical Israel, the question arises once again: when and why was this dialectic lost? Westermann makes the interesting observation that the biblical understanding of the human person (its *anthropology*) leads to the conclusion that "the existence of an individual without participation in a community (a *social*

---

10. Westermann, *Praise and Lament*, 264–265.

dimension) and without a relationship with God (a *theological* dimension) is totally inconceivable." Thus, the pattern of lament and praise presupposes "an understanding in which theology, psychology, and sociology have not yet been separated from each other."[11]

In the previous chapter we argued that the influence of Greek philosophy resulted in a distorted understanding of God, but Westermann's comment suggests that biblical anthropology suffered a similar fate since the exclusion of lament "is so thoroughly consistent with the ethic of Stoicism." In addition, he proposes that we need to take a critical look at the Reformation doctrine of justification by faith since this was "one-sidedly individualistic." Justification became narrowed down to the needs of the individual soul with the result that its social and political consequences were overlooked.[12] In subsequent centuries the *social* dimension of life was rediscovered in response to "the lamentation of the oppressed," triggering the great social revolutions of modern times. World Christianity, shaped by cultures beyond the West, can help us to face the challenge of the radical shift in our thinking which is urgently needed if we are to discover "a new and yet unrealized balance between the individual and society."[13]

I want to draw attention to a particular example of the manner in which the psalms of lament are capable of meeting specific pastoral needs in situations in which suffering threatens to overwhelm faith and to destroy the meaning of life itself. Douglas John Hall has argued that the dominant pathology of modern times is the anxiety of meaninglessness and emptiness. He points out that for well over a century this condition has been dramatically portrayed by

---

11. Westermann, 268; emphasis added.

12. This is precisely the kind of area in which the limitations of Western traditions in theology can be corrected by insights from Christians in the Majority World. For example, in a study entitled *The Amnesty of Grace: Justification by Faith from a Latin American Perspective*, Elsa Tamez writes, "[T]he abyss between the doctrine and the reality of our poor people allows the doctrine to remain floating in ambiguity, which in turn is conducive to its facile manipulation. . . . What does justification say to the poor indigenous peoples of Peru, Guatemala, Bolivia, or Mexico, who suffer both hunger and permanent discrimination? . . . If we accept that sin has to do with social reality, justification also has to be understood within that same horizon." (Nashville: Abingdon Press, 1993), 20–21.

13. Westermann, *Praise and Lament*, 269–270. Consider René Padilla's words at the Lausanne Congress in 1974: "The church is called to be here and now what God intends the whole of society to be. In its prophetic ministry it lays open the evils that frustrate the purpose of God in society; in its evangelization it seeks to integrate men into the purpose of God whose full realization is to take place in the Kingdom to come. Consequently, wherever the church fails as a prophet it also fails as an evangelist." "Evangelism and the World," in *Let the Earth Hear His Voice: International Congress on World Evangelization*, ed. J. D. Douglas (Minneapolis: Worldwide Publications, 1975), 137.

contemporary Western artists, writers and musicians, as well as by the critical analyses of psychology and sociology. Yet in a culture "determinedly fixed upon the utter meaningfulness of our entire exercise in progress, in happiness," the reality of *anomie* is continually denied and repressed, so that despair in life and the terror of death remain beneath the surface and "cannot admit" of themselves.[14] A Christianity which allows no place for either private or public lament consequently becomes complicit in this tragic denial and thereby contributes to a cover-up which deepens the hidden pain of those who suffer.

> Surely the first step toward a meaningful articulation of the Christian soteriology in our context would be for the churches to try to become spheres of truth, places where people can give expression to the anxiety of meaninglessness and emptiness – without being debilitated by the experience. It is unfortunate that our churches are, on the whole, places where people feel constrained to be even more hidden than usual.[15]

Among the psalms of lament none are more honestly expressive of the kind of condition Hall is describing than Psalm 88, which is a "singular exception" within the Psalter in that it contains no movement from lament to praise but comes to a bleak end with the profoundly honest statement that "darkness is my closest friend" (88:18). Here the outpouring of lament is met, as in the book of Lamentations, by *silence*. This tragic poem has proved to be an embarrassment to some commentators who contrive to discover a mitigating sign of hope where none exists. By contrast, Artur Weiser describes the psalm as uniquely "unrelieved by a single ray of comfort or hope." It is the profoundly moving testimony of someone who "feels God's eye gazing menacingly upon him through the mask of an incomprehensible calamity," following which "all his prayers prove unavailing in the face of God's terrible silence." Weiser concludes that Christians would be well advised, "when speaking of suffering, to come to terms with the thought that such agonies caused by hopeless loneliness

---

14. A key study of the individual, social and cultural consequences of the repression of the fear of death is Ernest Becker's great book, *The Denial of Death* (New York: Free Press, 1973). He sums up the tradition of thought that includes Augustine, Kierkegaard and Tillich as follows: "They saw that man could strut and boast all he wanted, but that he really drew his 'courage to be' from a god, from a string of sexual conquests, a Big Brother, a flag, a proletariat, and the fetish of money and the size of a bank balance" (56).

15. Hall, *Cross in Our Context*, 130–131.

belong to the sphere of the reality of God" and are part of human religious experience.[16]

In fact, in many of the situations to which we have referred earlier in this book, including the genocides in Europe and Africa, the unspeakable tragedy of the Congo, the sufferings of a war-torn Middle East, especially the plight of the peoples of Syria, and numberless similar contexts, the language of this psalm and the terrible silence at its end reflect reality in a way that provides assurance that even the deepest valley of human tragedy is recognized and given expression within the biblical tradition of faith. Carleen Mandolfo, in an article with the title "Psalm 88 and the Holocaust," observes that the very qualities which make this poem so difficult for many readers, namely, the absence of a response to the writer's anguished complaint, make it *"one of the most meaningful prayers that can be uttered"* in a context in which theology struggles to come to terms with the apparent senselessness of the world in the aftermath of the Holocaust.[17] She concludes, "Perhaps the silence is a good sign. . . . Perhaps even God recognizes the enormity of what has happened, and chooses not to answer so as not to belittle the suffering of the victims."[18]

This comment underlines what we have discovered earlier in this book, namely, that the biblical tradition of lament is of crucial importance with regard to the tragedies resulting from the violence of war, or from the destructive power unleashed in the natural world, when large numbers of people experience profound suffering *together*. However, Psalm 88 is an *individual* lament, which suggests that it has a particular resonance in relation to the pathologies of loneliness and meaninglessness which, as we have seen above, afflict so many people in the contemporary world. For example, the plight of the elderly in modern societies has long been recognized in the West, but in the era of globalization and with the spread of the values associated with free market capitalism across the earth, the world as a whole is "growing old" and traditional family solidarities are increasingly undermined. As Jeremy Seabrook puts it: "The compulsions that tore up an ancient peasantry from the earth of Britain are at work worldwide. They oblige the young and able to leave behind the old and weak as they move to seek work in factories, on

---

16. Artur Weiser, *The Psalms*, Old Testament Library (Philadelphia: Westminster John Knox, 1962), 586–587.

17. Carleen Mandolfo, "Psalm 88 and the Holocaust: Lament in Search of a Divine Response," *Biblical Interpretation* 15, no. 2 (2007): 7; emphasis mine.

18. Mandolfo, "Psalm 88," 19.

construction sites, in transport, as domestic servants, as vendors, drivers and security guards."[19]

Not only are the numbers of older people increasing exponentially, but diseases associated with ageing, such as dementia, bring previously unknown distress upon sufferers and place burdens of care upon family members at the very point in life where they have little strength, physically or emotionally, to cope with such situations. Aileen Barclay reads Psalm 88 from a context of "living with Alzheimer's disease" and affirms its profound importance as an "unresolved lament [which] has cathartic potential for those who suffer with the living bereavement of Alzheimer's disease and points towards the potentially transformative practice for churches."[20]

Barclay movingly describes her husband's descent into the shadowland of this disease and reads the text in light of that experience. Commenting on the cry of verse 5, "I am set apart with the dead," she says that the desperate struggle to "find ways through the maze of badly organized inadequate care saps energy, destroys hope, arouses anger, and increases confusion." Both sufferer and carer feel isolated, "set apart with the dead and cut off from care."[21]

A person of faith might expect that the exception to this sense of isolation and loneliness would be found within the worshipping life of the church, but here too the desperate cry of the psalmist that his *closest friends* kept their distance and appeared to regard him as "repulsive" (88:8) resonated with both sufferer and carer, not least because congregational life seemed determinedly fixed on praise and celebration. In addition, when the gospel is presented as demanding an intellectual grasp and affirmation of propositional truths, it becomes simply inaccessible to people who have lost the mental capacity to make such a response. Even to mention this is to expose the tragedy of the intellectualization of Christianity and the failure, particularly in certain evangelical traditions, to appreciate the importance of symbolism, of what occurs at the level of the subconscious, and of non-verbal forms of communication *by which spiritual life may be sustained.* Aileen Barclay's testimony presents a profound challenge to churches in what has been called the "age of loneliness": "In despair, confusion and the grief of living with my

---

19. Jeremy Seabrook, *A World Growing Old* (London: Pluto, 2003), 145. He discusses in detail the growing numbers of elderly people in areas of poverty across the Majority World and concludes: "The West grew rich before it grew old. The South is in the process of growing old before it has become rich" (14).

20. Aileen Barclay, "Psalm 88: Living with Alzheimer's," *Journal of Religion, Disability and Health* 16, no. 1 (2012): 88. See also her article "Lost in Eden: Dementia from Paradise," *Journal of Religion, Spirituality and Aging* 28, no. 1–2 (2016): 68–83.

21. Barclay, "Psalm 88," 90.

husband who once was a capable, intelligent, and gracious man, I remember the person whom I married and with whom I shared my life. I withdraw from my lively church, just unable to face people who keep telling me what a wonderful person my husband is."

Thus, Psalm 88, far from being a text to be avoided as an embarrassment, connects with an almost frightening reality to the silence and darkness experienced by a growing number of sufferers from the debilitating illnesses of old age. Indeed, it gives voice to a far wider circle of "voiceless" people, young as well as old, who live in the shadows at the margins of modern societies and who know perfectly well that the imagery which dominates mass culture, of happy, prosperous and beautiful people, represents a false ideology which denies and distorts reality and evades the critical issues of life and death.

How, then, might Christian churches become, in Hall's phrase, "spheres of truth"? Aileen Barclay helpfully suggests that they would acquire a greater understanding, and we may add, a deeper, Christlike compassion, if the stories of people who feel "set apart with the dead," and relatives who struggle to provide them with care, were heard regularly in public worship. In other words, communities of faith might increasingly reflect the pattern of the Bible in giving the voiceless a voice and in that process would discover not only the depths of pain experienced by people in their midst, but also recognize the extraordinary patience and undiminished love of carers for those who dwell in permanent darkness. Such care, expressed in utterly self-sacrificing love, might then come to be recognized as being of at least equal worth with the activities of those who go on short-term "mission trips" to exotic places. Caring for people with dementia is not short term and it is certainly not exotic, but precisely because it so often displays the inexhaustible compassion of Jesus its public recognition has the potential to enlarge and expand the churches' understanding of the *missio Dei* and to enable their own transformation into "spheres of truth."

Psalms and Hymns and Spiritual Songs

Earlier in this book we noticed the importance of music and song in contexts of deep human suffering. It is obvious that the Psalms were intended to be sung and we have seen that the book of Lamentations may itself have originated as a liturgy of lament amid the ruins of the city of Jerusalem. The instruction to the first Christian communities to "speak to one another with psalms, hymns and spiritual songs" (Eph 5:19) suggests that these groups continued to employ the patterns of worship which had been established across the centuries, especially in the synagogues, so that the relationship between lament and praise became part of the structure of Christian spirituality.[22] At the same time, new hymns reflecting the unique sense of the revolutionary change brought about by Christ were introduced in the gatherings of the earliest believers. We have glimpses of these new songs in praise of Christ scattered throughout the New Testament, most notably in the wonderful poem in Philippians 2:6–11 and in the descriptions of the praise of the redeemed, triumphant in heaven, in the book of Revelation. The hymns which burst out from the pages of John's Apocalypse constitute "new songs" in praise of Christ and of his reign over people "from every tribe and nation." It seems likely that these heavenly songs reflect the worshipping life of the terrestrial church toward the close of the first century since they "are full of traditional elements" and remind John's embattled hearers of their own regular worship "and particularly of the hymns they sing there." Klaus Wengst concludes: "In the solemnity of the liturgy the community hymns the power and glory of Christ; there it assures itself of this glory and anticipates a life under it which is free from the damage and oppression of the lordship exercised by others."[23]

And yet, even here at the climax of the biblical narrative we suddenly discover the resurfacing of the ancient question, "How long?" This time the language of lament is heard before the very throne of heaven, uttered by the martyrs whose blood was shed "because of the word of God and the testimony they had maintained" (Rev 6:9–11). Thus, the dialectic of praise and lament persists throughout the "last days," not least because, as the reply given to the martyrs indicates, the missionary calling of the body of Christ on earth is incomplete and its pursuit in a fallen world will result in yet further suffering and death! The church which praises Jesus and confesses him as the ultimate Lord will have need of the prayer of lament until the end finally comes.

What we have briefly touched upon here, and elsewhere throughout this book, is a *biblical theology of worship*. This leads to the conclusion that, in addition to the causes of the loss of lament in much contemporary Christianity already discussed, we must now add the lack of precisely such a theological foundation for public worship in much of the modern church. Christian assemblies are today frequently described as "praise gatherings" and it is not unusual to hear worship *defined* as sung praise. In many non-liturgical traditions the structure and content of worship now depends upon people

---

22. Walter Brueggemann comments that Col 3:12–17 "suggests that singing, along with forgiveness and thanks, is indeed a countercultural activity which marks the participants of the church and that distinguishes it from its cultural context." *A Glad Obedience: Why and What We Sing* (Louisville: Westminster John Knox, 2019), xiii–xiv.

23. Wengst, *Pax Romana*, 134.

who are described as "worship leaders." This almost amounts to a new office within the church and its emergence has meant that pastors have ceded aspects of their previous roles, stepping back to make space for people with musical gifts to take lead roles in public worship. I must stress that there is no objection in principle to this development which can be seen positively as a means of recognizing a far broader range of gifts than was ever possible when one man (and it was always a man) dominated the conduct of worship.

However, problems emerge, not because of the recognition of a wider range of gifts within the worshipping life of the church, but precisely because of the lack of grounding in the biblical tradition on the part of many of the people thrust into such positions. Equally significant is the limited experience of *life* and its tragedies and deep suffering in the case of young people who have yet to discover personal knowledge of the doubts and struggles encountered every day by members of congregations. Cut adrift from the dialectic spirituality of the Bible and from an earlier hymnology which expressed the whole gamut of human experience in language deeply grounded in biblical theology, worship may easily come to be shaped by wider cultural trends and end up focused almost entirely on the personal needs of individuals, oblivious to the reality of the idols which pose a threat to faithful discipleship and offering a spiritualized form of feel-good therapy.

On Wednesday, 13 March 1996, a deranged man armed with a gun walked into the primary school in the tranquil cathedral town of Dunblane in Scotland. He opened fire on anyone who came in sight and when the carnage was over, sixteen small children and their teacher lay dead. The shock of this tragedy reverberated across Scotland and throughout the world, and in its aftermath John Bell and Graham Maule wrote the following lines:

> There is a place prepared for little children,
> Those we once lived for, those we deeply mourn;
> Those who from play, from learning and from laughter
> Cruelly were torn.
>
> There is a place where hands which held ours tightly
> Now are released beyond all hurt and fear,
> Healed by that love which also feels our sorrow,
> Tear after tear.
>
> There is a place where all the lost potential
> Yields its full promise, finds its true intent;
> Silenced no more, young voices echo freely
> As they were meant.

There is a place where God will hear our questions,
Suffer our anger, share our speechless grief,
Gently repair the innocence of loving,
And of belief.

Jesus, who bids us be like little children,
Shields those our arms are yearning to embrace.
God will ensure that all are reunited;
There is a place.[24]

The authors stress that this song, together with its tune "Dunblane Primary," was not intended for congregational singing, but that when sung by a choir or a soloist it might create a space for reflection which would prove impossible "if everyone is involved in singing." This is a reminder that music and poetry may have a place in worship in their own right and that in some situations they may uniquely become the channels of healing and hope.

I want to digress at this point in order to reflect on the fact that, if some forms of Western Christianity lost contact with the biblical tradition of lament, this does not mean that it has been entirely absent from the wider culture. In the arts, in painting, literature, poetry and music, we discover again and again expressions of concern at the loss of God and the consequences of this for social cohesion, ethical principles and, perhaps most of all, for the source of meaning in human existence. During the last century the absence of God in the modern West was deeply felt by many sensitive people, a fact reflected in classic works of poetry, art and music now regarded as among the greatest in history.[25]

Consider, for example, the Seventh Symphony of the Russian composer Dmitri Shostakovich, known as "The Leningrad" on account of its having been written and first performed in that city during a terrible siege as the invading German army cut off an entire urban population from the rest of the world in the depths of a bone-chilling Russian winter. The tragedies which unfolded in that beleaguered city hardly bear imagining, yet during those desperate months

---

24. John L. Bell and Graham Maule, "There Is a Place," in *When Grief Is Raw: Songs for Times of Sorrow and Bereavement* (Glasgow: Wild Goose Publications, 1997), 92–95, and *The Last Journey* (London: SPCK, 2018). Copyright © 1997 WGRG, c/o Iona Community, Glasgow, Scotland. Reproduced by permission. www.wildgoose.scot.

25. Terry Eagleton comments: "Whereas modernism experiences the death of God as a trauma, an affront, a source of anguish as well as a cause for celebration, postmodernism does not experience it at all." *Culture and the Death of God*, 186. I am reminded of the words of young people spoken to a colleague of mine in eastern Germany: "We had forgotten that we had forgotten God."

Shostakovich completed this extraordinary symphony. I first heard this music while studying in Aberdeen and its power simply overwhelmed me. I knew little then concerning its context, but it was immediately obvious that it depicted the horror of war, the deep tragedy of the suffering and death which results from it, yet somehow still managed to retain hope for the coming of a different kind of world. Later, I researched the life and times of Shostakovich and discovered, among many other things, his remarkable concern for the Jewish people and his deep love of their music. At a time when a virulent wave of anti-Semitism was sweeping through the Soviet Union, Shostakovich said that the Jewish people had symbolic significance since "All man's defencelessness was concentrated in them." His love of Jewish folk music and his deep and courageous compassion for the Jewish people is reflected at many points in his compositions, but most remarkable is the fact that Shostakovich found inspiration for the Leningrad Symphony in reading the Hebrew Bible.

> I began writing [the Seventh Symphony] having been deeply moved by the psalms of David ... the psalms were the impetus. ... David has some marvellous words on blood; God takes revenge for blood. He doesn't forget the cries of victims, and so on. When I think of the psalms I become agitated. And if the psalms were read before every performance of the Seventh, there might be fewer stupid things written about it.[26]

There is a deep irony here; at a time when the churches of the West began losing contact with the biblical tradition of the lament, a Russian composer who never professed faith was deeply moved by the Psalms and became the medium for the transmission of their message in both the honest outpouring of grief and the surprising survival of hope. This music has reached a global audience, giving voice to millions of people suffering the agonies and trauma of a post-war world because it possesses a peculiar power to touch the very depths of the human soul. Shostakovich described his symphonies as being like "tombstones," because "too many of our people died and were buried in places unknown to anyone, not even their relatives." When words fail us and

---

26. Dmitri Shostakovich, *Testimony: The Memoirs of Shostakovich, As Related to and Edited by Solomon Volkov* (London: Hamish Hamilton, 1979), 140. This book caused much controversy when first translated into English and its reliability was challenged. It is now generally accepted as an accurate record of Volkov's conversations with the composer, although questions may always be asked as to exactly what "edited" means.

we are left dumb by the mystery of suffering, music of this kind has the power to speak to the heart and renew the "courage to be."[27]

Credible Testimony in a Broken World

When I shared with a circle of close friends that I was attempting to write this book and mentioned the title, one of them replied suggesting that I must be "referring to Yeats's terrifying poem." In fact, I had no thought of Yeats's work and the inspiration for my title came, as I have described in the preface, from a completely different source. However, having had Yeats's famous lines in his "Second Coming" pointed out to me, I am struck by the relevance of this fascinating, mysterious composition in relation to my subject and I will use it as the basis for these concluding reflections. Some of the poet's lines are now very famous and have been cited many times in modern literature:

> Things fall apart; the centre cannot hold;
> Mere anarchy is loosed upon the world.

Or again,

> The best lack all conviction, while the worst
> Are full of passionate intensity.

My first encounter with this poem was in Nigeria where, struggling to understand the cultural world within which I had now made my home, I came across the work of the great Nigerian writer Chinua Achebe. His celebrated novel *Things Fall Apart* obviously takes its title from Yeats's poem, the opening lines of which were reproduced on that book's first page. Achebe movingly described the impact of colonialism and missionary Christianity upon his traditional Igbo society, and in one of the most challenging passages of this tragic narrative of the collapse of Igbo culture and community he places this lament in the mouth of one of his leading characters: "The white man is very clever. He came quietly and peaceably with his religion. We were amused at his foolishness and allowed him to stay. Now he has won our brothers, and

---

27. On classical music and world Christianity, see David Martin, "Christianity and 'Western Classical' Music (1700–2000)," in *The Wiley Blackwell Companion to World Christianity*, ed. Lamin Sanneh and Michael McClymond (Chichester: Wiley Blackwell, 2016), 350–358. This volume is an indispensable reference work for the study of world Christianity. A striking example of the power of Shostakovich's music to bring healing and hope to depressed people can be found in Stephen Johnson, *How Shostakovich Changed My Mind* (Honiton: Notting Hill Editions, 2018).

our clan can no longer act like one. He has put a knife on the things that held us together and we have fallen apart."[28]

Those lines will find resonance among many tribal, or "primal," peoples across the world wherever small-scale societies have existed for thousands of years, self-sustaining, living close to other creatures and to the natural world, but now overwhelmed by the impact first of colonial powers and then by the spread of what came to be called modernity. The economic historian Karl Polanyi described this period in world history as one in which a "great transformation" occurred by which an older world was swept away and replaced by one based on a new creed in which transcendent values were exchanged for purely material ones. Human beings came to be defined as naturally acquisitive and self-interested creatures whose desires must not only be released from the restraints of an outdated morality but actually stimulated and encouraged. Polanyi wrote that "a new way of life spread over the planet with a claim to universality unparalleled since the age when Christianity started out on its career, only this time the movement was on a purely material level."[29] He described the devastation visited upon cohesive, traditional societies in Europe during the Industrial Revolution, and went on to discuss the unspeakable tragedies which occurred across the southern hemisphere as this new ideology clashed with the ancient values of tribal communities. A market economy was "forced upon an entirely differently organized community; labor and land are made into commodities," a change so profound and far-reaching that it resulted in "the liquidation of every and any cultural institution in an organic society."[30] Polanyi described the impact of this revolution on Asia, particularly in India, before noting the specific case of the forced land allotment made to American native peoples in 1887, a move "which benefitted them individually, according to our financial scale of reckoning. *Yet the measure all but destroyed the race in its physical existence – the outstanding case of cultural degeneration on record.*"[31]

Notice then that although Yeats's poem was obviously concerned with the deepening cultural crisis in the Western world, it has come to have a universal relevance wherever the acids of modernity have done their work. Yeats was, of course, far from alone in sensing a deep malaise in modern societies and

---

28. Chinua Achebe, *Things Fall Apart*, in *The African Trilogy* (London: Everyman's Library, 2010), 124.

29. Karl Polanyi, *The Great Transformation: The Political and Economic Origins of Our Time* (Boston: Beacon, 1957), 136.

30. Polanyi, *Great Transformation*, 167.

31. Polanyi, 168; emphasis added.

his profound unease found powerful expression in all the arts. Indeed, other poets, most notably Walt Whitman, memorably expressed a similar anxiety:

> Wandering, yearning, with restless explorations,
> With questionings, baffled, formless, feverish, with never happy
>   hearts.
> With that sad incessant refrain, wherefore unsatisfied soul?
> Whither O mocking life?
> Ah, who shall soothe these feverish children?
> Who justify these restless explorations?
> Who speak the secret of the impassive earth?

These lines gained currency far beyond poetry-reading circles when set to music in Vaughan Williams's magnificent *Sea Symphony* and to listen to them in that context is a deeply moving experience. What both Whitman and Yeats, among very many others, were articulating was the *sense of an ending*. A long period of history during which, as we have seen, the world was transformed by earth-shaking developments and was moving toward its terminus, and there was great uncertainty and deep anxiety concerning what might follow it. Yeats's "Second Coming" is profoundly ambiguous and has left interpreters debating what it means ever since. While using Christian imagery, he suggests that the emerging "revelation" will be utterly unlike the incarnation of Christ and that, with Christianity having run its course, the future may be shaped by a "rough beast" slouching "towards Bethlehem to be born." Is this a warning that as the global crisis deepens, a figure, or perhaps a system, will emerge to exercise coercive power on the international stage, bringing order at the cost of freedom amid the chaos of an Easter Saturday culture on course for complete collapse?

By contrast, Whitman is far more hopeful:

> After the seas are all crossed,
> After the great captains have accomplished their work,
> After the noble inventors,
> Finally shall come the poet worthy of that name,
> The true son of God shall come singing his songs.

In other words, when human technological skill and creativity has reached its limit, and the "wondering, yearning" and questioning increases to a point at which it becomes a universal longing for answers to the riddle of human existence, *then* the cries of all the ages will receive their answer in what sounds like (to use biblical language) the coming of the kingdom! Whitman seems to leave us in little doubt about this in words which in Vaughan Williams's hands are transformed into one of the greatest moments in all symphonic music:

Bathe me O God in Thee, mounting to Thee,
I and my soul to range within range of Thee.
O Thou transcendent.[32]

This is the historical context within which world Christianity, as indicated in the final column of our diagram, has come into existence, and the crucial question is: how can the witness of this global movement become credible in relation to the situation we have just described? The answer to this question obviously lies beyond the scope of this present book, but I propose that, whatever else the emergent movement will need if it is to meet the challenge of these times, the pattern of praise and lament which we have seen to be embedded within the biblical tradition must become a core part of its spirituality, worship, theology and, indeed, its very identity. Such a transformation will be costly and difficult, involving something like a reconversion, especially for Christians in the Western world who have been so profoundly socialized within a pervasive culture which assumes that endless "progress" is normal.

Walter Brueggemann has described how all of us are *scripted* by this culture which then shapes our values, aspirations and practices. The dominant worldview since the "great transformation" of modern times is "the script of therapeutic, technological, consumer militarism that permeates every dimension of our common life." This all-pervasive culture is internalized through the processes of nurture, education and the stimulation of desires, and "all of us, across the spectrum, are powerfully inducted into it."[33] This *script* shapes modern politics and education and is propagated and reinforced by a battery of powerful channels of oral and visual communication that is unprecedented in human history. We have earlier mentioned the role of visual imagery in enforcing Roman propaganda in the ancient world, but today the power of mass media in closing down alternative ways of thinking about the world and locking us into the orthodoxy of the ideology of the free market is literally overwhelming. Yet while this *script* promises us so much, its offer of safety and happiness is increasingly exposed as an illusion and it becomes ever clearer that it is leading us toward social and planetary death. Brueggemann concludes that the task of a world church at this critical juncture of human history is to "bear witness to the failure of that script and to relinquish the world evoked" by it, while at the same time engaging in the "steady, patient,

---

32. My source for the Whitman poem here is the CD booklet accompanying a recording of Vaughan Williams's *A Sea Symphony* by the BBC Symphony Orchestra and the Philharmonia Chorus conducted by Leonard Slatkin. BBC *Music Magazine* 224.

33. Walter Bruegemann, *Mandate to Difference: An Invitation to the Contemporary Church* (Louisville: Westminster John Knox, 2007), 192.

intentional articulation of an alternative script that we testify can make us safe and joyous."[34]

Can we discern a mysterious providence in the fact that the very process of globalization has itself triggered reactions which create new possibilities for the credible articulation of the alternative script of the gospel? For example, the migratory movements of modern times, whereby huge numbers of people from across the southern hemisphere have moved northwards in search of economic survival, have begun to transform the social and religious character of many European and North American cities. Gerri ter Haar describes how the tens of thousands of African Christians now living in Europe "consider that God has given them a unique opportunity to spread the good news among those who have gone astray." She concludes that the reversal of roles implied by an African mission to Europe "stands many conventional ideas on their head," so that "the rise of African and other non-Western congregations in London, Paris, Frankfurt, and even in Moscow, is nothing less than a new phase in the religious history of Europe."[35]

In this new era of Christian history the most urgent issue confronting the universal body of Christ concerns "the challenge of being the Holy Catholic or Universal church." An interconnected world "brings us into better informed solidarity with Christians around the globe," while "burning issues for the historical and emerging churches find commonality on every continent."[36] The critical issue is, can Christians in Europe and North America, so long used to belonging to *sending* churches, with all the assumptions which accompany such a status, now accept their new location at the margins of the dynamic centres of fresh theological thinking and of new understandings of Christian identity and witness in a pluralist world? And will they hear and listen to the voices coming from "below" with searching challenges to many of their long-embedded assumptions concerning belief, discipleship and worship?[37]

---

34. Bruegemann, *Mandate to Difference*, 195.

35. Gerrie ter Haar, *Halfway to Paradise: African Christians in Europe* (Cardiff: Cardiff Academic Press, 1998), 3. See Andrew Walls's important discussion "Toward a Theology of Migration" in his book *Crossing Cultural Frontiers*, 49–61. He concludes that the Great European migrations of the imperial age, by which the nations of the southern hemisphere were changed, have now gone into reverse so that "for the first time in many centuries there is the possibility of returning to something like the conditions of early Christianity with its different converted lifestyles equally essential to the welfare of the one culturally diverse church" (60).

36. John Bell and Charles Robertson, "Foreword," *Hymns of Glory, Songs of Praise* (Norwich: Canterbury Press, 2008), vii.

37. See Soong-Chan Rah, *The Next Evangelicalism: Freeing the Church from Western Cultural Captivity* (Downers Grove, IL: InterVarsity Press, 2009). Written of the situation in the USA his analysis is relevant to Western Christianity in general: "We lift up those who are

In chapter 5 we heard Jean-Marc Ela's "African cry" and his penetrating question as to which God "people in the West believe in." Ela asked, it will be remembered, "What is the good news for those who live in dominating societies?" In other words, how do we articulate the gospel for people who benefit from the existing structures of globalization and what might conversion mean in such contexts? The same searching issue has been at the forefront of the prophetic work of theologians in Latin America where the suffering and oppression of so many people continues to go unnoticed by rich Christians who are, according to Jon Sobrino,

> submerged in the "sleep of inhumanity." People do not want to acknowledge or face up to the reality of a crucified world, and even less do we want to ask ourselves what is our share of responsibility for such a world. The world of poverty is truly the great unknown. It is surprising that the First World can know so much and yet ignore what is so fundamental about the world in which we live.[38]

If that ignorance is overcome and both the sufferings of the poor and the complicity of the rich in the global systems which create such injustice are recognized, then the question of Psalm 137 will become an urgent priority for us: "How can we sing the songs of the LORD in a strange land?" How must our worshipping practice and content be transformed in the light of our growing knowledge of the realities of our times? I propose that the praises of world Christianity today must connect with the pain and suffering of people, while at the same time articulating the shift in our understanding of the *suffering of God in Christ* as we have discussed this in the previous chapter. Brian Wren is a theologian and poet who has contributed fresh songs for worship which beautifully express both of these dimensions.

> Great God, in Christ you call our name
> And then receive us as your own,
> Not through some merit, right, or claim,
> But by your gracious love alone.
> We strain to glimpse your mercy-seat
> And find you kneeling at our feet.

---

the haves, believing that our church life will be complete if we emulate these models of success. Instead, if we are to be liberated from the Western, white captivity of the church, we need to begin learning the stories of the have-nots and learn from those who dwell in the theology of suffering" (155).

38. Sobrino, quoted in Daniel Bell Jr., *Liberation Theology after the End of History: The Refusal to Cease Suffering* (London: Routledge, 2001), 175.

Then take the towel, and break the bread,
And humble us, and call us friends.
Suffer and serve till all are fed
And show how grandly love intends
To work till all creation sings,
To fill all worlds, to crown all things.

Great God, in Christ you set us free
Your life to live, your joy to share.
Give us your Spirit's liberty
To turn from guilt and dull despair
And offer all that faith can do
While love is making all things new.[39]

In 2010 I returned to Nigeria with my wife Joyce to teach at the Theological College of Northern Nigeria and at the Jos Evangelical Theological Seminary. We arrived in the city of Jos at a time when tensions between Christians and Muslims were running high following previous outbreaks of serious inter-communal violence. We were to stay in a guest house close to the city centre, which meant that I would need to drive to Bukuru outside the city each day to the beautiful campus of TCNN. One Monday morning we heard stories that were circulating of a clash in a particular district of the city on the previous day, but it appeared to be limited to that locality and unlikely to spark any wider violence. However, half way through the morning I was in worship in the college chapel when my mobile phone rang and the voice at the other end said: "Whatever you are doing now, stop it and get back to the guest house! The barricades are going up on the roads – if you get stopped it is likely to be by a 'Christian' group and you should be able to get through." I also learned that the Nigerian army was about to impose an immediate curfew and I knew perfectly well the risks of being seen to breach that order. Heart beating furiously, I raced back down an eerily empty dual carriageway into the city, and just made it through the gates of the guest house as the soldiers appeared on the street outside.

The curfew remained in place for most of that week, so we were confined to the guest house, listening night after night to the sound of incessant gunfire close by with no knowledge of what was actually happening. When the sounds

---

39. Three verses from the text of "Great God, your love has called us here" (Brian Wren, born 1936), ©1975, 1995 Stainer & Bell Ltd, 23 Gruneisen Road, London, N3 1DZ, England, www.stainer.co.uk. Used by permission from "Piece Together Praise" (Stainer & Bell, 1996). All rights reserved.

of firing eventually began to fade, the night watchmen reported that trucks had rumbled past the gates in the early morning filled with corpses heading for mass burial and it became clear that Jos had been convulsed by a major tragedy. When the curfew was finally lifted we emerged from the relative security of the guest house to witness the aftermath of the trouble on the streets where people walked in a kind of daze, still anxious that a small spark could ignite a renewed conflagration.

I relate this experience not as a kind of "missionary travel story" but because of something that I discovered in the days following our confinement. Walking on a nearby street a few days later, I met a woman with a small stall trading in mangoes, bananas and tinned fish. I greeted her and we began talking about the troubles and the tragedy of this city, promoted as "the Home of Peace and Tourism" yet now rent apart by ethnic and religious divisions. She drew my attention to a pile of leaflets which she was distributing to all her customers, calling on the women of Jos to come together *in order to lament before God the tragedy which was transforming this city into a place of mutual mistrust, hatred and murderous violence.* I gratefully took the leaflet and discovered it appealing to the precedent of Jeremiah:

> Call for the wailing women to come;
>> send for the most skilful of them.
> Let them come quickly
>> and wail over us
> till our eyes overflow with tears
>> and water streams from our eyelids.
> The sound of wailing is heard from Zion:
>> "How ruined we are!
>> How great is our shame!
> We must leave our land
>> because our houses are in ruins." (Jer 9:17–19)

The actual event promoted by these leaflets took place after we had departed from Nigeria, with thousands of Christian women gathering for a day expressing penitence, lament and fervent prayer for "the peace of the city." The conversation with that humble African woman and her ability to connect the words of Jeremiah with the contemporary tragedies of a city which sits astride the fault line between Christianity and Islam in Africa had a profound impact on me and has remained with me ever since. Of course, traditional African culture is much closer to the biblical world of Jeremiah than is that of the modern West; the "call for the wailing women" is easily understood by people who expect that even a good death will be mourned with public, bodily expressions of lament. Therefore, it was no surprise that the violence seen in Jos, which appeared senseless and out of control, triggering passions which resulted in a kind of madness, should result in a *communal lament*. Like Jeremiah, many of these women could say they had seen death climb in "through our windows" and "cut off the children from the streets" (Jer 9:21), and this demanded penitence and lament.

As we saw earlier, the practice of lament is an integral aspect of African Christianity. However, it is important to note that this is far more than simply a passive expression of regret or pain, a kind of safety valve which releases emotional pressure. Those women who gathered in Jos believed that lament could bring about change, that it had the power to move God to respond, and thus it was the basis of the hope that a new, transformed world was possible. At the conclusion of his book *Born from Lament*, Emmanuel Katangole comments that the public expression of pain and loss throughout Africa, far from being a flight from political reality, actually represents the *birthpangs of an alternative social and political vision for the future of the continent*. Lament "deepens and intensifies engagement with the world of suffering," inviting those who practise it into "deeper political engagement, while at the same time reframing and reconstituting the very nature and meaning of politics." Those who lament the brokenness, wickedness and hatred which so often seem to dominate the existing world glimpse

> the shape of a new politics in the midst of Africa's politics of greed and self-seeking power. It is not simply political reform that they are interested in, but a thorough theological reinvention of politics. . . . They have been led to – and they invoke – a totally new vision of society. Their advocacy and initiatives *reflect the shape of the new world, which now breaks forth within the shell of the old world as both radical critique of and an alternative to the politics of military alliances and economic greed.*[40]

Do we not discover here one of the "burning issues" which brings us into "better informed solidarity with Christians around the globe"? And does this not suggest that the recovery of lament in the churches of Europe and North America is urgently required, not only because of their internal pastoral needs, but (perhaps even more importantly) as an expression of their credibility in witness to the gospel in a broken and unjust world? There are

---

40. Katangole, *Born from Lament*, 262–263.

clear indications of a renewed interest in the biblical lament in regard to the suffering of individuals, but this can only be a first step in a movement which must eventually lead to the re-embedding of lament in corporate worship and spirituality.[41]

Notice that the text in Jeremiah of which mention was made above demands the communal lament not as an end in itself, but as a means to cause "our eyes to overflow" with tears. That is to say, the lament is intended to *shatter the protective shell which enables us to look on global tragedies and not be heartbroken!* Not for nothing is Jeremiah known as the "weeping prophet," and his tears set him apart from both the hard-faced men of power, who insisted that all was well, and the smiling throngs in the temple whose celebratory praise concealed the horrible reality of their complicity in "business as usual."

Nearly twenty years ago I published a small book with the title *Crying in the Wilderness: Evangelism and Mission in Today's Culture*. I beg the reader's indulgence if I quote from the introduction to that study:

> If Christians are to heed the tears of those lost in the wilderness . . .
> then I suggest that they will not themselves be strangers to tears.
> In this respect their true model . . . [will be] the Christ who was
> "a man of sorrows, acquainted with grief." Alas, far too much
> Christian proclamation has been done by men with dry eyes.
> Looking out over a sea of tears such preachers have retained a
> dignified detachment which bears an uncanny likeness to the
> religious orthodoxy of the ecclesiastical police who descended on
> John the Baptist from Jerusalem. Preaching of this kind achieves
> nothing, except to further alienate the poor and needy and to
> confirm their impression that religious people are insufferable
> hypocrites whose self-righteousness marks them out as people
> to be avoided.[42]

In the two decades since those words were written I venture to suggest that the world has grown darker and multiple crises now threaten the well-being of rising and future generations on Planet Earth. How can Christianity appear as the source of a credible hope in the twenty-first century if it knows only

---

41. With regard to renewed interest in lament in relation to personal suffering, see J. Todd Billings, *Rejoicing in Lament: Wrestling with Incurable Cancer and Life in Christ* (Grand Rapids, MI: Brazos, 2015); Kelly M. Kapic, *Embodied Hope: A Theological Meditation on Pain and Suffering* (Downers Grove, IL: IVP Academic, 2017); and especially Alain Emerson, *Luminous Dark* (Edinburgh: Muddy Pearl, 2017).

42. David W. Smith, *Crying in the Wilderness: Evangelism and Mission in Today's Culture* (Carlisle: Paternoster, 2000), xi.

the language of praise while the world burns? Who will listen to its claim to be the bearer of a message of peace when that peace is narrowed down to the sphere of the individual soul and those claiming it remain silent as a new nuclear arms race comes over the horizon, posing a far greater threat to the created world and all life on it than was known during the earlier cold war? And even if, using the tools of successful marketing and the technologies of modern communication, the downward curve of church attendance in Europe were to be reversed, what distinguishes such a church from expanding business enterprises when the ethical practice of its members becomes indistinguishable from the consumerist patterns dominating the wider culture and resulting in the pathologies of meaninglessness and nihilism discussed earlier in this chapter? The refusal of lament at such a time as this would be a symptom of apostasy on the part of the comfortable and wealthy church of the Western world, and all the more so since the example of Christianity at its growing edges in the Majority World was available and offered the possibility of biblical renewal, of a new and deeper grasp of the gospel, and the opportunity to display before all nations the transformative love and unity which, according to Jesus, is the crucial evidence that will convince the world that the Father has sent the Son.

The message of the gospel of Jesus Christ, crucified, buried and raised from death, brings hope and joy into the darkness of our world. It enables us to say with Paul, "If God is for us, who can be against us?" (Rom 8:31). The assurance of God's mercy, love and compassion is grounded on the astonishing fact that in Christ God has experienced the deepest depths of suffering, enduring humiliation, abandonment and the terrors of hell. We repeat here the words of Richard Bauckham and Trevor Hart: "The cross, where Jesus drank to the dregs the cup of God-forsaken death, is not a stage in the upward ascent of human history, but a descent to its depths *in order to bring God into those depths.*"[43] This is the deepest foundation of Christian praise and joyful celebration since it gives birth to the hope that the turning point of all the ages does indeed lie behind us. God's long-promised *shalom* has broken into the present and through the power of the resurrection and the gift of the Holy Spirit is already at work, transforming this world and moving it toward God's future. This is cause for loud, ecstatic celebration; it was the motivating force compelling the early Christians to sing "psalms and hymns and spiritual songs," and to do so in ways that were "robust and emotive."[44] Yet Christian hope must be

---

43. Bauckham and Hart, *Hope against Hope*, 40; emphasis added.
44. Brueggemann, *Glad Obedience*, xiii.

distinguished from triumphalism since the continuing reality of suffering and death may not be ignored or suppressed, and the removal of all the causes of grief, loss and weeping remains in the future.

Jürgen Moltmann beautifully expresses the nature of Christian hope when he writes that the resurrection of Jesus "is not merely a consolation . . . in a life that is full of distress and doomed to die, but it is also God's contradiction of suffering and death, of humiliation and offence, and of the wickedness of evil." Hope brings consolation to the broken-hearted *in* their suffering, but it is also "the protest of the divine promise *against* suffering." The hope which flows from the resurrection "must be declared to be the enemy of death and of a world that puts up with death."[45] The faith of the Bible is not, and can never be, a passive, private affair, but rather it drives those who confess it out into the world in solidarity with the lost, the despised, the hopeless and homeless.

> That is why faith, wherever it develops into hope, causes not rest but unrest, not patience but impatience. It does not calm the unquiet heart, but is itself this unquiet heart in man. Those who hope in Christ can no longer put up with reality as it is, but begin to suffer under it. Peace with God means conflict with the world, for the goad of the promised future stabs inexorably into the flesh of every unfulfilled present.[46]

Which is why the whole catholic church must recover a biblical theology and practice of worship, rejoicing in the faithfulness and love of the God who bears the name of Immanuel, while weeping over the still unredeemed-ness of the present, and continuing to pray that the kingdom may soon come in its fullness. Meantime, the community of the people of God drawn from all nations will point the world toward the promised future in which God will "reconcile to himself all things, whether things on earth or things in heaven, by making peace through his blood, shed on the cross" (Col 1:20). *Maranatha –* "Our Lord, come!"

---

45. Jürgen Moltmann, *Theology of Hope: On the Ground and the Implications of a Christian Eschatology* (London: SCM, 1967), 21.

46. Moltmann, *Theology of Hope*, 21.

For Reflection

> Then I looked and heard the voice of many angels, numbering
> thousands upon thousands, and ten thousand times ten thousand.
> They encircled the throne and the living creatures and the elders.
> In a loud voice they sang:
>
> "Worthy is the Lamb, who was slain,
> to receive power and wealth and wisdom and strength
> and honour and glory and praise!"
> Then I heard every creature in heaven and on earth and under the
>   earth and on the sea, and all that is in them, singing:
> "To him who sits on the throne and to the Lamb
> be praise and honour and glory and power,
>   for ever and ever!"
> The four living creatures said "Amen," and the elders fell down
>   and worshipped. (Rev 5:11–14)

[The book of] Revelation represents an important moment at the very beginning of Christianity, one rooted in the history of the people of Israel and in the prophetic-apocalyptic movement within which the Jesus movement, the apostolic mission, and the first Christian communities take their rise. Revelation draws together and transforms the Jewish and Judeo-Christian apocalyptic tradition; within the church its function is one of critique of, and resistance to, the Hellenization of Christianity and its authoritarian and patriarchal institutionalization. Over the long run, it was disregard of Revelation that opened the way for the incorporation of the church into the dominant imperial system and the construction of an authoritarian Christendom. To retrieve Revelation is to retrieve a fundamental dimension of the Jesus movement and of the origins of Christianity. Revelation is not an isolated book, one belonging to a sectarian or desperate tiny group, but rather a universal book that presses for radical reform of the church and a new way of being Christian in the world.[47]

---

47. Pablo Richard, *Apocalypse: A People's Commentary on the Book of Revelation* (Eugene, OR: Wipf & Stock, 2008), 3.

Appendix 1

Paul's Missionary Theology

In the discussion of the life and work of Paul in chapter 4 I suggested that he faced a difficult tension between his "core conviction" concerning the significance of Christ in the history of the human race, on the one hand, and the reality of the condition of the world during the first century, on the other. This would suggest that Paul's ministry reflected a pattern similar to the dialectic which we have earlier noticed in regard to the Old Testament and the experience of biblical Israel. In order to illustrate this I want to consider the extraordinary nature of the apostle's *hope* with regard to what the gospel might achieve in a world governed by Roman power and ideology, and the apparent *frustration* of that hope as the result of Paul's arrest, imprisonment and eventual execution.

In chapter 15 of the letter to the Romans Paul declares that he had "fully proclaimed the gospel of Christ" from Jerusalem to Illyricum and that "there is no more place for me to work in these regions" (15:19–23). This amounts to an astonishing claim that the foundational work of mission throughout the eastern empire had been completed; the seed of the gospel had been planted and was bearing fruit in urban centres across the vast area Paul had traversed and, since his ambition was to push back new frontiers, to preach "where Christ was not known," he now turned his eyes westward to the ends of the earth in Spain. His desire to at last visit Rome, which had been signalled at the start of this letter, is now revealed to be not an end in itself, but a means to make possible the creation of a staging post on the way to fulfilling his ultimate ambition to "go to Spain."

Spain represented the "end of the world" both in the obvious geographical sense, but also as a wild region in which resistance to Roman power and civilization remained strong despite endless wars designed to pacify the "barbarian" population. In the century before Christ there had been particularly brutal Roman military campaigns on the Iberian peninsula, including the sacking of the town of Termantia with the slaughter of ten thousand inhabitants and the betrayal of an agreement with another town which was followed by

131

the massacre of men, women and children. Both Julius Caesar and Pompey fought on Spanish soil, imposing taxation and enlistment into the legions on conquered peoples. Robert Jewett describes a continuing pattern of "local resistance, cultural conflict, and imperial exploitation" which "had lasted for more than two and a half centuries before Paul began to make plans for a mission to Spain."[1]

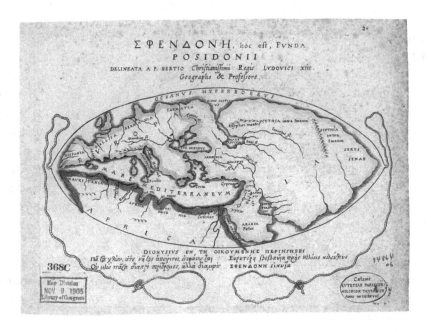

Figure A.1: Posidonius's Map of the World. First Century BCE. Library of Congress, Geography and Map Division.

Since Spain was located at the extreme western end of the strip maps of antiquity, and since the peoples who lived there were notoriously resistant to Graeco-Roman culture and influence, it was the logical destination for the apostle to the Gentiles. Paul's ambition to preach Christ in that region was also stimulated by the promise of Isaiah 66:18–21 that the "distant islands" and peoples from "all the nations" would stream into the kingdom of God,

---

1. Jewett, *Romans: A Commentary*, Hermeneia, 77–78. This magnificent commentary treats the letter to the Romans as "designed to prepare the way for the complicated project of the Spanish mission" and discusses both Paul's strategy in mission and the context of Spain in great detail.

so that by assisting him in this plan the followers of Jesus in Rome would play their part in the eschatological purpose of God and the ushering in of the long-promised *shalom*. Jewett describes the whole argument of the letter to the Romans, including the great central chapters 9–11 which wrestle with the mystery of God's purposes in human history, as intended to secure the support of the house churches in Rome, "thus serving the ultimate purpose of divine righteousness in regaining control of a lost and disobedient world." The overarching argument of the epistle connects salvation with "cosmic transformation, theology with ethics, faith with tolerance," and Jewett concludes that if this central thrust is properly grasped, the letter to the Romans "might still provide a basis for achieving its original vision: to bring 'all the peoples' (Rom 15:11) to praise the One whose gospel can still restore our eroded and fractured world to its intended wholeness."[2]

Having said all of this and glimpsed the vastness of Paul's holy ambition, we (and I suspect the original hearers of this letter) are shocked by his announcement that the Spanish mission must wait since his immediate priority is to return to Jerusalem! There is surely a huge sense of anticlimax at this point as the exciting project involving the breaking of entirely fresh ground in mission is immediately subordinated to a strategy which involves Paul retracing his steps and returning to the original heartland of the faith of Jesus Christ. The great vision which he wants the Roman believers to share is focused on the west, yet he plans to go east! The unfinished, or not even begun, task lies in Spain, yet he wishes to go back across areas in which he has already said "there is no more place for me to work in these regions"!

Clearly, the decision to return to Jerusalem, a journey which involved very great risks (15:30–31), must be related to theological and missiological convictions that were of absolutely fundamental importance for the apostle Paul. *What were these convictions?* They were related to unfinished business with regard to a promise which Paul had made at the very commencement of his ministry, to "continue to remember the poor" (Gal 2:10). Concealed within that cryptic phrase we discover convictions regarding the nature of the new community which God is bringing into being through the work of Christ and the socio-economic and political character of that community. The "remembrance of the poor" is far more than the kind of one-off charitable act with which we are familiar; it took tangible, concrete form in the shape of "the collection" which had been a core component of Paul's entire ministry

---

2. Robert Jewett, "Following the Argument of Romans," in *The Romans Debate*, ed. Karl P. Donfried, revised and expanded ed. (Peabody, MA: Hendrickson, 1991), 276–277.

and which had, by this time, accumulated from contributions made among all the churches which had sprung from his labours. That collection, which now consisted of a substantial sum of money, was both the expression of Christian solidarity and love and a visible sign that the new world was breaking into the harsh social and economic realities of the old one, destroying ethnic and racial barriers and demonstrating the power of the cross to break the idolatrous hold of Mammon and heal the fractures which divided the human family.

We have noticed the presence and power of *money* in the ancient world, both as an economic reality and as a means of propagating the Roman, imperial ideology. Dieter Georgi suggests that Paul taught his Gentile converts that the acceptance of the message of Jesus's resurrection from the dead resulted in their integration within "a unique, worldwide community; the people of God of the new creation," and that this change of status carried obligations, including the sharing of resources both locally and between peoples. The "collection" was thus "the evidence of their will toward partnership; it constituted the 'sign of [their] communion' with the poor saints in Jerusalem (Rom 15:26)."[3] The collection, we may say, was the concrete evidence that "the dividing wall of hostility" between Jew and Gentile had been abolished through the reconciling power of the cross and that Christ had indeed become "our peace," creating "one new man out of the two" (Eph 2:14–18). From the side of Gentile converts, the collection expressed indebtedness to their Jewish brothers and sisters and gratitude that they had now come to share the promises of God to his covenant people, while from the other side, the *acceptance* of the offering would signal the embrace of these "other sheep" on the basis of their faith in the crucified Christ. This explains precisely why this journey to Jerusalem was fraught with danger since, amid a rising tide of militant Jewish nationalism in Palestine, it took place "in full view of orthodox Jewry and conservative Jewish believers" and was liable to be understood by them as a provocative "demonstration of the fact that the traditional biblical and Jewish eschatological expectation was being reversed." As Georgi says, the fact that Gentile believers claimed to be "equal members with the people of the covenant without prior compliance with the requirements of proselytes, was itself a provocation."[4]

The failure of the "collection" to achieve the outcome which had been hoped for and the huge consequences of this for Paul's life and mission compels us to ask whether, in the highly charged context of Jerusalem, the substantial

---

3. Dieter Georgi, *Remembering the Poor: The History of Paul's Collection for Jerusalem* (Nashville: Abingdon Press, 1992), 117.

4. Georgi, *Remembering the Poor*, 117.

monetary gift was itself provocative in the eyes of conservative Jews? The experience of missionary work from Europe and North America among poor people across the Majority World during the past two centuries has taught us that cultures rarely meet on level terms, so that cross-cultural encounters, especially in contexts of imperial and colonial power, are characterized by political, social and economic asymmetry. As a result, what may be intended from one side as an act of mercy and solidarity can be interpreted by recipients as masking unspoken, concealed intentions designed to undermine local cultures. Did conservative Jews in Jerusalem facing hunger during a serious famine interpret the offering of a large sum of money from Gentile followers of Jesus as a form of *bribery*, making "conversion" more likely? We cannot know the answer to this question, but our experience of the pitfalls and misunderstandings that arise in precisely such situations suggests at least that such an explanation is possible.[5]

So we ask again, why did Paul place at risk the exciting project of the Spanish mission by insisting on the priority of returning to the seething cauldron of Jerusalem, knowing full well that this placed his very life in danger? I suggest that the answer to this question is related to the *credibility of his preaching and its promise of peace and reconciliation through the cross of Jesus Christ.* How could he go to Spain with the announcement of forgiveness, healing and freedom if, in the regions where his ministry had been completed, the promise of *shalom* was being contradicted by the re-emergence of the old racial and religious divisions and hatreds? The relationship between Jews and Gentiles within the body of Christ was a kind of litmus test for the truthfulness of the claims of the gospel; could it really bring into being a new human family in which the old hostilities were transcended and abolished, or was this in reality simply wishful thinking which would come to grief in the face of the harsh reality of a divided, broken world that never really changes? So crucial was this issue for Paul that mission at the new frontiers had to wait until love, unity and respect for difference could be concretely demonstrated as the outcome of the gospel in the previous heartlands.

---

5. See the helpful diagrams concerning asymmetry between cultures in Carlos Cardoza-Orlandi, *Mission: An Essential Guide* (Nashville: Abingdon Press, 2002), 113–115. On the fate of the collection, Wayne Meeks writes: "The collection effort proved disastrous. If it was accepted at all by the Jerusalem group, it must have been in such a way as to imply the second-class status of Gentile Christians. Even so, the presence of Paul with representatives of the Gentile churches was a provocation to some faction in the Jewish community, leading to Paul's arrest and the end of his career." *The First Urban Christians: The Social World of the Apostle Paul* (New Haven: Yale University Press, 1983), 110.

It hardly needs to be said that two thousand years later, and with the long, frequently tragic history of Christendom behind us, the issues which confronted Paul in the first century remain as urgent and difficult as ever for the world Christian movement. Dieter Georgi's description of the significance of the collection for the poor of Jerusalem points toward the precise nature of the challenge facing Christianity in the globalized world of today:

> The collection of funds for Jerusalem in Paul's interpretation transforms the idea of an economy geared toward growth of production and profit as the Hellenistic economy already was. . . . Increase of wealth for him needs to be common wealth. The money collected for Jerusalem grows also, but into a universal divine worship. The money involved becomes a social force, a gift from community to community. It is intended to forge the vitality of the community it is given to. Here obedience and simple kindness are blended. *In this process the subjugation of the universe under the Rich One who became poor has begun, and the unification of humanity has been initiated.*[6]

As we know, Paul made the journey to Jerusalem with the result that the serious disturbance caused by his presence within the city led to his arrest and imprisonment. The great vision to evangelize Spain never became reality and although Paul came at last to Rome, it was as a chained prisoner facing a capital charge during the reign of Nero and with the disciples of Jesus in that city divided in their attitudes toward him. Can there be a clearer example of the tension between the core belief of the gospel and the counter-testimony arising from the painful realities of a still broken world? When Paul writes with his own hand the pathetic plea, "Remember my chains" (Col 4:18), he surely reflects a personal struggle to come to terms with his situation in which his own prayers must have included the ancient questions, "Why?" and "How long?"[7]

---

6. Georgi, *Remembering the Poor*, 153; emphasis added. Elsewhere Georgi observes that "justification is not important merely between God and the individual but comes about and manifests itself in the interrelatedness of God, the world, and humanity." Righteousness which mirrors God's own "is not a pious possession of the individual. It is the liberty of integrated human beings, incorporated into a body of justifying grace and love" (159).

7. Tom Wright has suggested that Paul may have been temporarily released from custody, providing an opportunity for him to visit Spain, a journey which Clement, bishop of Rome in the late first century, may refer to when he wrote that the apostle "reached the farthest limits of the West." However, even if this possibility were to be accepted, such a visit would fall far short of the fulfilment of Paul's missionary ambition for Spain as this is described in Romans 15. See Tom Wright, *Paul: A Biography* (London: SPCK, 2018), 392–393.

Appendix 2

A Global Chorus Singing New Songs

The purpose of this appendix is to provide a few examples of the kinds of voices emerging from the growing edge of the world Christian movement across the southern hemisphere. The selections are obviously somewhat arbitrary, but it is hoped that they illustrate both the freshness and the profoundly challenging nature of contributions to Christian theology and practice which are reshaping the church worldwide. Justo González has already been quoted a number of times in this book, but we hear him again at this point since his reflections on theology from a Hispanic perspective are both trenchant and serve as a good introduction to the statements which follow.

> [T]he reformation of the twentieth century is taking place within the context of the macroevents of our time, and several of its characteristics reflect those macroevents.
>
> One characteristic of our macroreformation is that voices are being heard from quarters that have not been the traditional centers of theological enquiry, and from people who have not been among traditional theological leaders. [M]ission theoreticians of the past . . . expected theology to continue being what it was, for the meaning of the gospel was fully understood by the sending churches, and all that the younger ones had to do was to continue proclaiming the same message. At best, these younger churches were to recast the message in terms of their own culture. The surprise of our generation has been that the younger churches have provided insights into the meaning of the gospel and the mission of the church that the older churches sorely needed. From Asia, Africa, and Latin America, as well as from ethnic minorities in North America and other places, and from women all over the world, have come stunning visions of the meaning of the gospel, and a number of theologians in the traditional centers

of theological learning have seen the value of these insights. The dialogue that has resulted means that theology will never be the same again.[1]

———

The first voice we hear is from *Native America*. This is important both because it represents a significant movement among the aboriginal populations of North America, but also because the concerns expressed here are very similar to those which are heard across the world among Christians whose religious and cultural heritage has been shaped by traditional or primal religions.

> Ours . . . is the history of peoples who lived at least 13,000 years on this continent before Columbus arrived. Our people created cultures based on spiritual beliefs which bound them together in a life of simplicity and balance with each other and with the earth.
>
> When we read the Gospel, we must read it as *Native people*, for this is who we are. We can no longer try to be what we think the dominant society wants us to be. As Native, Catholic people, we must set out with open minds and hearts; then we will encounter Jesus Christ. . . . We have to go beyond the *white gospel* in order to perceive its truth.
>
> When we do this, we shall meet Jesus as our brother and recognize him as one who has been with us all along as the quiet servant, the one who has strengthened us through these centuries. Then we will know that the cry of Jesus Christ from the cross was the cry of our people at Wounded Knee, Sand Creek and other places of mass death of our people. He was our companion during these years of our invisibility in this society. This same Jesus is the one who challenges us to grow beyond ourselves. This is the challenge of evangelization. If we take up the challenge we shall sense that he is with us and be glad. This is the heart and core meaning of the Gospel.[2]

———

1. González, *Mañana*, 48.

2. Marie Therese Archambault, "Native Americans and Evangelization," in *Native and Christian: Indigenous Voices on Religious Identity in the United States and Canada*, ed. James Treat (London: Routledge, 1996), 132–133.

The second voice is from Asia and comes from the Japanese theologian Kosuke Koyama:

> This religion called Christianity is, it seems to me, most interested in teaching people, but not interested in being taught by people. It speaks to people, but it does not listen to them. I do not think Christianity in Asia for the last 400 years has really listened to the people. It has ignored people. Ignoring *things* is not so bad, but ignoring *people* is serious. It has listened to its bishops, theologians and financial sponsors. But it really has not listened to the people.
>
> Christianity has been busy planning mission strategy – this campaign and that crusade. People have become the object of evangelization since it is understood by Christians that people are "automatically" living in the darkness, untrustworthy, wicked, adulterous and unsaved, while believers are "automatically" living in the light, good, not lustful, and saved. The "teacher complex" expresses itself in a "crusade complex." What a comfortable arrangement for the believers! What an irresponsible and easygoing theology![3]

The third voice is African. It is that of Lamin Sanneh, describing the momentous nature of the changes taking place on that continent.

> [T]o understand the changing face of Christianity today, we must forget our modern rationalism, our proud confidence in reason and science, our restless search after wealth and power and after an earthly kingdom. We must enter sympathetically into the mood of populations disillusioned with old assurances, as well as with the new call to the pursuits of secular preeminence. The new Christians are standing, as it were, between the shipwreck of the old order and the tarnished fruits of self-rule of the new, finding all the dreams of a worldly utopia shattered by betrayal, war, vanity, anarchy, poverty, epidemics, and endemic hostility. They are seeking refuge in the justification of the righteous kingdom, flocking to the churches because the old fences of what used to be have crumbled. They are inspired and comforted by the narratives of ancient scripture, throwing themselves upon the mercy and

---

3. Kosuke Koyama, *Three Mile an Hour God* (London: SCM, 1979), 52.

goodness of God and upon one another's charity. They are living in the reality of a fellowship established, a cause vindicated, a judgement fulfilled, and a hope rekindled. The dramatic response of compressed, preindustrial societies of the non-Western world to Christianity has opened a new chapter in the annals of religion.[4]

———

The voice representative of South America has to be that of Archbishop Óscar Romero. He spoke for the final time in the chapel of a cancer hospital in San Salvador on 24 March 1980. The gospel reading was John 12:23–26 and Romero commented on a grain of wheat needing to die in order to bear fruit. He quoted from the documents of Vatican II:

> "We are warned that it profits a man nothing if he gains the whole world and lose himself. . . . The expectation of a new earth must not weaken but rather stimulate our concern for cultivating this one. For here grows the body of a new human family, a body which even now is able to give some kind of foreshadowing of the new age. . . . Dear brothers and sisters, let us view these matters at this historic moment with that hope, that spirit of giving and sacrifice. Let us all do what we can. We can do something, at least have a sense of understanding and sympathy."
>
> *As the archbishop began celebration of the eucharist, a shot rang out and he fell mortally wounded. He died within minutes in the nearby hospital.*[5]

———

4. Lamin Sanneh, "Conclusion: Current Transformation of Christianity," in *The Changing Face of Christianity: Africa, the West, and the World*, ed. Lamin Sanneh and Joel Carpenter (New York: Oxford University Press, 2005), 222–223.

5. Archbishop Óscar Romero, *Voice of the Voiceless* (Maryknoll, NY: Orbis, 1985), 192–193.

Bibliography

Achebe, Chinua. *The African Trilogy*. London: Everyman's Library, 2010.

Allen, Leslie C. *A Liturgy of Grief: A Pastoral Commentary on Lamentations*. Grand Rapids, MI: Baker Academic, 2011.

Archambault, Marie Therese. "Native Americans and Evangelization." In *Native and Christian*, edited by James Treat, 132–153.

Balch, David L. "Paul's Portrait of Christ Crucified (Gal. 3:1) in Light of Paintings and Sculptures of Suffering and Death in Pompeiian and Roman Houses." In Balch and Osiek, *Early Christian Families*, 84–108.

Balch, David L., and Carolyn Osiek, eds. *Early Christian Families in Context: An Interdisciplinary Dialogue*. Grand Rapids, MI: Eerdmans, 2003.

Barclay, Aileen. "Lost in Eden: Dementia from Paradise." *Journal of Religion, Spirituality and Aging* 28, no. 1–2 (2016): 68–83.

———. "Psalm 88: Living with Alzheimer's." *Journal of Religion, Disability and Health* 16, no. 1 (2012): 88–101.

Bauckham, Richard. *The Bible in the Contemporary World: Exploring Texts and Contexts – Then and Now*. London: SPCK, 2016.

———. *Jesus and the Eyewitnesses: The Gospels as Eyewitness Testimony*. Grand Rapids, MI: Eerdmans, 2006.

Bauckham R., and T. Hart. *Hope against Hope: Christian Eschatology in Contemporary Context*. London: Darton, Longman & Todd, 1999.

Becker, Ernest. *The Denial of Death*. New York: Free Press, 1973.

Bell, Daniel Jr. *Liberation Theology after the End of History: The Refusal to Cease Suffering*. London: Routledge, 2001.

Bell, John L., and Graham Maule. *When Grief Is Raw: Songs for Times of Sorrow and Bereavement*. Glasgow: Wild Goose, 1997.

Bell, John, and Charles Robertson. "Foreword." *Hymns of Glory, Songs of Praise*. Norwich: Canterbury Press, 2008.

Billings, J. Todd. *Rejoicing in Lament: Wrestling with Incurable Cancer and Life in Christ*. Grand Rapids, MI: Brazos, 2015.

Bonhoeffer, Dietrich. *Letters and Papers from Prison*. London: Fontana, 1959.

Brueggemann, Walter. *Abiding Astonishment: Psalms, Modernity and the Making of History*. Louisville: Westminster John Knox, 1991.

———. "The Costly Loss of Lament." In *Psalms*, edited by Patrick D. Miller, 98–111.

———. *A Glad Obedience: Why and What We Sing*. Louisville: Westminster John Knox, 2019.

———. *Hopeful Imagination: Prophetic Voices in Exile*. Philadelphia: Fortress, 1986.

———. *Israel's Praise: Doxology against Idolatry and Ideology*. Philadelphia: Fortress, 1988.

———. *Living toward a Vision: Biblical Reflections on Shalom*. New York: United Church Press, 1976.

———. *Mandate to Difference: An Invitation to the Contemporary Church*. Louisville: Westminster John Knox, 2007.

———. *The Prophetic Imagination*. Philadelphia: Fortress, 1978.

———. *Spirituality of the Psalms*. Minneapolis: Fortress, 2002.

———. *Texts That Linger, Words That Explode*. Minneapolis: Fortress, 2000.

———. *Theology of the Old Testament: Testimony, Dispute, Advocacy*. Minneapolis: Fortress, 1997.

Buber, Martin. *The Prophetic Faith*. New York: Macmillan, 1949.

Burrows, William R. "Conversion: Individual and Cultural." In Burrows, Gornik and McLean, *Understanding World Christianity*, 109–126.

Burrows, William, Mark Gornik and Janice McLean, eds. *Understanding World Christianity: The Vision and Work of Andrew F. Walls*. Maryknoll, NY: Orbis, 2011.

Camus, Albert. *The Myth of Sisyphus*. London: Penguin, 1975.

———. *The Rebel*. Harmondsworth: Penguin, 1971.

Cardoza-Orlandi, Carlos. *Mission: An Essential Guide*. Nashville: Abingdon Press, 2002.

Carter, Warren. *Matthew and the Margins: A Socio-Political and Religious Reading*. London: T&T Clark, 2000.

Cassidy, Richard J. *Christians and Roman Rule in the New Testament: New Perspectives*. New York: Crossroad, 2001.

———. *Jesus, Politics and Society: A Study in Luke's Gospel*. Maryknoll, NY: Orbis, 1978.

———. *John's Gospel in New Perspective: Christology and the Realities of Roman Power*. Maryknoll, NY: Orbis, 1992; 2nd ed., Eugene, OR: Wipf & Stock, 2015.

———. *Paul in Chains: Roman Imprisonment in the Letters of St. Paul*. New York: Crossroad, 2001.

———. *Society and Politics in the Acts of the Apostles*. Maryknoll, NY: Orbis, 1987.

Chesterton, G. K. *Orthodoxy*. Project Gutenberg eBook. Last modified 26 September 2005. Accessed 2 October 2018. www.gutenberg.org/cache/epub/130/pg130-images.html.

Cocker, Mark. *Rivers of Blood, Rivers of Gold: Europe's Conflict with Tribal Peoples*. London: Pimlico, 1999.

Collier, Jane. *The Culture of Economism: An Exploration of Barriers to Faith-As-Praxis*. Frankfurt: Peter Lang, 1990.

Collier, Jane, and Rafael Esteban. *From Complicity to Encounter: The Church and the Culture of Economism*. Harrisburg, PA: Trinity Press International, 1998.

Cragg, Kenneth. *Christianity in World Perspective*. London: Lutterworth, 1968.

Cranfield, C. E. B. *Romans*. Vol. 1. International Critical Commentary. Edinburgh: T&T Clark, 1975.

Davidson, Robert. *The Courage to Doubt: Exploring an Old Testament Theme*. London: SCM, 1983.

Donfried, Karl P. *The Romans Debate*. Revised and expanded ed. Peabody, MA: Hendrickson, 1991.

Dostoevsky, Fydor. *The Idiot*. Harmondsworth: Penguin, 1955.

Douglas, J. D., ed. *Let the Earth Hear His Voice: International Congress on World Evangelization*. Minneapolis: Worldwide Publications, 1975.

Dyrness, William, and Veli-Matti Kärkkäinen, eds. *Global Dictionary of Theology: A Resource for the Worldwide Church*. Downers Grove, IL: IVP Academic, 2008.

Eagleton, Terry. *Culture and the Death of God*. New Haven: Yale University Press, 2015.

Ela, Jean-Marc. *African Cry*. Eugene, OR: Wipf & Stock, 2005.

———. *From Charity to Liberation*. London: Catholic Institute for International Relations, 1984.

———. *My Faith as an African*. Nairobi: Acton, 2001.

Ellington, Scott. *Risking Truth: Reshaping the World through Prayers of Lament*. Eugene, OR: Pickwick, 2008.

Elliott, Neil. *The Arrogance of Nations: Reading Romans in the Shadow of Empire*. Minneapolis: Fortress, 2008.

———. "Strategies of Resistance and Hidden Transcripts in the Pauline Communities." In Horsely, *Hidden Transcripts*, 97–122.

Emerson, Alain. *Luminous Dark*. Edinburgh: Muddy Pearl, 2017.

Essler, Philip, ed. *Christianity for the Twenty-First Century*. Edinburgh: T&T Clark, 1998.

Fee, Gordon. *Philippians*. IVP New Testament Commentary. Downers Grove, IL: InterVarsity Press, 1999.

Fretheim, Terence. *The Suffering of God: An Old Testament Perspective*. Philadelphia: Fortress, 1984.

Freyne, Sean. *Jesus: A Jewish Galilean – A New Reading of the Jesus Story*. London: T&T Clark, 2004.

Frick, Peter. "Nietzsche: The Archetype of Pauline Deconstruction." In Frick, *Paul*, 15–37.

Frick, Peter, ed. *Paul in the Grip of the Philosophers: The Apostle and Contemporary Continental Philosophers*. Minneapolis: Fortress, 2013.

Fujimura, Makoto. *Silence and Beauty: Hidden Faith Born of Suffering*. Downers Grove, IL: InterVarsity Press, 2016.

Gener, T. D., and L. Bautista. "Theological Method." In Dyrness and Kärkkäinen, *Global Dictionary of Theology*, 889–894.

Georgi, Dieter. *Remembering the Poor: The History of Paul's Collection for Jerusalem*. Nashville: Abingdon Press, 1992.

———. *Theocracy in Paul's Practice and Theology*. Minneapolis: Fortress, 1991.

Goatley, David Emmanuel. *Where You There? Godforsakenness in Slave Religion*. Maryknoll, NY: Orbis, 1996.

González, Justo L. *Mañana: Christian Theology from a Hispanic Perspective*. Nashville: Abingdon Press, 1990.

Gorringe, Timothy J. "After Christianity?" In Essler, *Christianity*, 261–274.

Graham, Stephen. *Vertical: The City from Satellites to Bunkers.* London: Verso, 2016.

Gregory, Brad S. *The Unintended Reformation: How a Religious Revolution Secularized Society.* Cambridge, MA: Belknap Press of Harvard University, 2012.

Gutiérrez, Gustavo. *On Job: God-Talk and the Suffering of the Innocent.* Maryknoll, NY: Orbis, 1987.

Haar, Gerrie ter. *Halfway to Paradise: African Christians in Europe.* Cardiff: Cardiff Academic Press, 1998.

Hall, Douglas John. *The Cross in Our Context: Jesus and the Suffering World.* Minneapolis: Fortress, 2003.

Harari, Yuval Noah. *Homo Deus: A Brief History of Tomorrow.* London: Vintage, 2017.

———. "The New Opium of the Masses." *The Guardian,* 8 May 2018, 10–11.

Hastings, Adrian, ed. *The Oxford Companion to Christian Thought; Intellectual, Spiritual and Moral Horizons of Christianity.* Oxford: Oxford University Press, 2000.

Heltzel, Peter Goodwin. *Resurrection City: A Theology of Improvisation.* Grand Rapids, MI: Eerdmans, 2012.

Hengel, Martin. *Crucifixion in the Ancient World and the Folly of the Message of the Cross.* Philadelphia: Fortress, 1977.

Heschel, Abraham. *God in Search of Man: A Philosophy of Judaism.* London: Souvenir, 2009.

Hobsbawm, Eric. *Age of Extremes: The Short Twentieth Century, 1914–1991.* London: Abacus, 1995.

Hochschild, Adam. *King Leopold's Ghost: A Story of Greed, Terror and Heroism in Colonial Africa.* London: Pan, 2012.

Hoekendijk, J. C. *The Church Inside Out.* London: SCM, 1967.

Holland, Tom. *Dominion: The Making of the Western Mind.* London: Little, Brown, 2019.

Hollingdale, R. J., ed. *A Nietzsche Reader.* Harmondsworth: Penguin, 1977.

Horsley, Richard A., ed. *Hidden Transcripts and the Arts of Resistance: Applying the Work of James C. Scott to Jesus and Paul.* Atlanta: Society for Biblical Literature, 2004.

Janzen, J. Gerald. *Job.* Interpretation: A Bible Commentary for Teaching and Preaching. Atlanta: John Knox, 1985.

Jenkins, Philip. *The Lost History of Christianity: The Thousand-Year Golden Age of the Church in the Middle East, Africa and Asia – And How It Died.* New York: HarperOne, 2008.

———. *The New Faces of Christianity: Believing the Bible in the Global South.* New York: Oxford University Press, 2006.

———. *The Next Christendom: The Coming of Global Christianity.* New York: Oxford University Press, 2002.

Jervis, L. Ann. "Reading Romans 7 in Conversation with Postcolonial Theory: Paul's Struggle toward a Christian Identity of Hybridity." In Christopher Stanley, *Colonized Apostle,* 95–109.

Jewett, Robert. "Following the Argument of Romans." In Donfreid, *Romans Debate,* 276–277.

———. *Romans*. Basic Bible Commentary. Nashville: Abingdon Press, 1988.

———. *Romans: A Commentary*. Hermeneia. Minneapolis: Fortress, 2007.

Johnson, Stephen. *How Shostakovich Changed My Mind*. Honiton: Notting Hill Editions, 2018.

Judt, Tony. *Postwar: A History of Europe since 1945*. London: Vintage, 2010.

Kahl, Brigitte. "Galatians and the 'Orientalism' of Justification by Faith: Paul among Jews and Muslims." In Christopher Stanley, *Colonized Apostle*, 206–222.

———. *Galatians Reimagined: Reading with the Eyes of the Vanquished*. Minneapolis: Fortress, 2010.

Kapic, Kelly M. *Embodied Hope: A Theological Meditation on Pain and Suffering*. Downers Grove, IL: IVP Academic, 2017.

Katangole, Emmanuel. *Born from Lament: The Theology and Politics of Hope in Africa*. Grand Rapids, MI: Eerdmans, 2017.

———. *The Journey of Reconciliation: Groaning for a New Creation in Africa*. Maryknoll, NY: Orbis, 2017.

———. *The Sacrifice of Africa: A Political Theology for Africa*. Grand Rapids, MI: Eerdmans, 2011.

Katangole, Emmanuel, and Chris Rice. *Reconciling All Things: A Christian Vision of Justice, Peace and Healing*. Downers Grove, IL: InterVarsity Press, 2008.

Keller, Catherine. "The Love of Postcolonialism: Theology in the Interstices of Empire." In Keller, Nausner and Rivera, *Postcolonial Theologies*, 221–242.

Keller, Catherine, Michael Nausner and Mayra Rivera, eds. *Postcolonial Theologies: Divinity and Empire*. St. Louis: Chalice, 2011.

Kitamori, Kazoh. *Theology of the Pain of God*. London: SCM, 1966.

Koyama, Kosuke. *Three Mile an Hour God*. London: SCM, 1979.

Kreitzer, Larry. *Striking New Images: Roman Imperial Coinage and the New Testament World*. Sheffield: Sheffield Academic Press, 1996.

Kuhn, Karl Allen. *Luke the Elite Evangelist*. Collegeville, MN: Liturgical, 2010.

Lee, Nancy C. *Lyrics of Lament: From Tragedy to Transformation*. Minneapolis: Fortress, 2010.

Lewis, Alan. *Between Cross and Resurrection: A Theology of Holy Saturday*. Grand Rapids, MI: Eerdmans, 2001.

Lieven, Anatol. *Pakistan: A Hard Country*. London: Penguin, 2002.

Lopez, Davina. *Apostle to the Conquered: Reimagining Paul's Mission*. Minneapolis: Fortress, 2008.

———. "Visualizing Significant Otherness: Reimagining Paul(ine Studies) through Hybrid Lenses." In Christopher Stanley, *Colonized Apostle*, 74–94.

Lorke, Mélisande, and Dietrich Werner, eds. *Ecumenical Visions for the 21st Century: A Reader for Theological Education*. Geneva: WCC, 2013.

Lovell, John Jr. *Black Song: The Forge and the Flame*. New York: Macmillan, 1972.

Mandolfo, Carleen. "Psalm 88 and the Holocaust: Lament in Search of a Divine Response." *Biblical Interpretation* 15, no. 2 (2007): 1–20.

Marchal, Joseph, ed. *The People beside Paul: The Philippian Assembly and History from Below*. Atlanta: Society for Biblical Literature, 2015.

Martin, David. "Christianity and 'Western Classical' Music (1700–2000)." In Sanneh and McClymond, *Wiley Blackwell Companion*, 350–358.

Mauser, Ulrich. *The Gospel of Peace: A Scriptural Message for Today's World*. Louisville, KY: Westminster John Knox, 1992.

Mazower, Mark. *Dark Continent: Europe's Twentieth Century*. London: Penguin, 1988.

McGuckin, John. "Greek Theology, 4th–6th Centuries." In Hastings, *Oxford Companion*, 278–283.

Meeks, Wayne. *The First Urban Christians: The Social World of the Apostle Paul*. New Haven: Yale University Press, 1983.

Milbank, John, Slavoj Žižek and Creston Davis. *Paul's New Moment: Continental Philosophy and the Future of Christian Theology*. Grand Rapids, MI: Brazos, 2010.

Miller, Patrick D., ed. *The Psalms: The Life of Faith*. Minneapolis: Fortress, 1995.

Moltmann, Jürgen. *The Crucified God: The Cross of Christ as the Foundation and Criticism of Christian Theology*. London: SCM, 1974.

———. *Experiences of God*. Philadelphia: Fortress, 1980.

———. *Theology of Hope: On the Ground and the Implications of a Christian Eschatology*. London: SCM, 1967.

Myers, Ched. "Mark 13 in a Different Imperial Context." In Vincent, *Mark*, 164–175.

Nanos, Mark D. "Out-Howling the Cynics: Reconceptualizing the Concerns of Paul's Audience from His Polemics in Philippians 3." In Marchal, *People beside Paul*, 183–221.

Oakes, Peter. *Reading Romans in Pompeii: Paul's Letter at Ground Level*. London: SPCK, 2009.

O'Connor, Kathleen. *Lamentations and the Tears of the World*. Maryknoll, NY: Orbis, 2002.

Ott, Craig, and Harold Netland, eds. *Globalizing Theology: Belief and Practice in the Era of World Christianity*. Nottingham: Apollos, 2007.

Padilla, René. "Evangelism and the World." In Douglas, *Let the Earth*, 116–146.

Parry, Robin. *Lamentations*. Two Horizons Old Testament Commentary. Grand Rapids, MI: Eerdmans, 2010.

Pelikan, Jaroslav. *Jesus through the Centuries: His Place in the History of Culture*. New York: Harper & Row, 1985.

Phillips, J. B. *The New Testament in Modern English*. London: Geoffrey Bles, 1960.

Polanyi, Karl. *The Great Transformation: The Political and Economic Origins of Our Time*. Boston: Beacon, 1957.

Poon, Michael Nai-Chiu. "The Rise of Asian Pacific Christianity and Challenges for the Church Universal." In Lorke and Werner, *Ecumenical Visions*, 65–72.

Price, S. R. F. *Rituals and Power: The Roman Imperial Cult in Asia Minor*. Cambridge: Cambridge University Press, 1986.

Prunier, Gerard. *Africa's World War: The Congo, the Rwandan Genocide, and the Making of a Continental Catastrophe*. Oxford: Oxford University Press, 2011.

Rah, Soong-Chan. *The Next Evangelicalism: Freeing the Church from Western Cultural Captivity*. Downers Grove, IL: InterVarsity Press, 2009.

Richard, Pablo. *Apocalypse: A People's Commentary on the Book of Revelation*. Eugene, OR: Wipf & Stock, 2008.

Roberts, Elizabeth, and Ann Shukman, eds. *Christianity for the Twenty-First Century: The Life and Work of Alexander Men*. London: SCM, 1996.

Roetzel, Calvin. *Paul: The Man and the Myth*. Edinburgh: T&T Clark, 1999.

Romero, Archbishop Óscar. *Voice of the Voiceless*. Maryknoll, NY: Orbis, 1985.

Rowe, C. Kavin. *World Upside Down: Reading Luke–Acts in the Graeco-Roman Age*. Oxford: Oxford University Press, 2009.

Rubinstein, Richard L. *After Auschwitz: Radical Theology and Contemporary Judaism*. New York: Bobbs-Merrill, 1966.

Sanneh, Lamin. *Whose Religion Is Christianity? The Gospel beyond the West*. Grand Rapids, MI: Eerdmans, 2003.

Sanneh, Lamin, and Joel Carpenter, eds. *The Changing Face of Christianity: Africa, the West, and the World*. New York: Oxford University Press, 2005.

Sanneh, Lamin, and Michael McClymond, eds. *The Wiley Blackwell Companion to World Christianity*. Chichester: Wiley Blackwell, 2016.

Schreiter, Robert. *The New Catholicity: Theology between the Global and the Local*. Maryknoll, NY: Orbis, 2004.

Seabrook, Jeremy. *A World Growing Old*. London: Pluto, 2003.

Shenk, Wilbert, ed. *Enlarging the Story: Perspectives on Writing World Christian History*. Maryknoll, NY: Orbis, 2002.

Shostakovich, Dmitri. *Testimony: The Memoirs of Shostakovich, as Related to and Edited by Solomon Volkov*. London: Hamish Hamilton, 1979.

Smith, David W. *Crying in the Wilderness: Evangelism and Mission in Today's Culture*. Carlisle: Paternoster, 2000.

———. *Moving toward Emmaus: Hope in a Time of Uncertainty*. London: SPCK, 2007.

———. "Theology as a Voice for the Voiceless: Jean-Marc Ela's *African Cry*." *Theological College of Northern Nigeria Research Bulletin* 52 (March 2010): 19–29.

Snyder, Timothy. *Bloodlands: Europe between Hitler and Stalin*. London: Vintage, 2011.

Standhartinger, Angela. "Letter from Prison as Hidden Transcript: What It Tells Us about the People at Philippi." In Marchal, *People beside Paul*, 107–140.

Stanley, Brian. *Christianity in the Twentieth Century: A World History*. Princeton, NJ: Princeton University Press, 2018.

Stanley, Christopher, ed. *The Colonized Apostle: Paul through Postcolonial Eyes*. Minneapolis: Fortress, 2011.

Stearns, Jason K. *Dancing in the Glory of Monsters: The Collapse of the Congo and the Great War of Africa*. New York: Public Affairs, 2011.

Steiner, George. *Real Presences: Is There Anything in What We Say?* London: Faber & Faber, 1991.

Stern, J. P. *Nietzsche*. London: Fontana/Collins, 1978.

Tamez, Elsa. *The Amnesty of Grace: Justification by Faith from a Latin American Perspective*. Nashville: Abingdon Press, 1993.

Thiselton, Anthony. *1 Corinthians: A Shorter Exegetical and Pastoral Commentary*. Grand Rapids, MI: Eerdmans, 2006.

Tillich, Paul. *The Shaking of the Foundations*. Harmondsworth: Penguin, 1949.

Treat, James, ed. *Native and Christian: Indigenous Voices on Religious Identity in the United States and Canada*. London: Routledge, 1996.

Vanhoozer, Kevin. "'One Rule to Rule Them All?' Theological Method in an Era of World Christianity." In Ott and Netland, *Globalizing Theology*, 85–126.

Villanueva, Federico. *Lamentations: A Pastoral and Contextual Commentary*. Carlisle: Langham Global Library, 2016.

Vincent, John, ed. *Mark: Gospel of Action – Personal and Community Responses*. London: SPCK, 2006.

Walls, Andrew, F. "Christian Expansion and the Condition of Western Culture." Henry Martyn Lecture 1985 in *Changing the World*, 14–25. Bromley: MARC Europe, n.d.

———. *The Cross-Cultural Process in Christian History*. Edinburgh: T&T Clark, 2002.

———. *Crossing Cultural Frontiers: Studies in the History of World Christianity*. Maryknoll, NY: Orbis, 2017.

———. *The Missionary Movement in Christian History: Studies in the Transmission of Faith*. Edinburgh: T&T Clark, 1996.

Weiser, Artur. *The Psalms*. Old Testament Library. Philadelphia: Westminster John Knox, 1962.

Wengst, Klaus. *Pax Romana and the Peace of Jesus Christ*. London: SCM, 1987.

Westermann, Claus. *The Living Psalms*. Grand Rapids, MI: Eerdmans, 1989.

———. *Praise and Lament in the Psalms*. 2nd ed. Atlanta: John Knox Press, 1981.

Williams, Stephen. *The Shadow of the Antichrist: Nietzsche's Critique of Christianity*. Grand Rapids, MI: Baker Academic, 2006.

Wilson, Derek. *Hans Holbein: Portrait of an Unknown Man*. London: Phoenix, 1996.

Wren, Brian. *What Language Shall I Borrow? God-Talk in Worship: A Male Response to Feminist Theology*. London: SCM, 1989.

Wright, Christopher. *The Mission of God: Unlocking the Bible's Grand Narrative*. Downers Grove, IL: InterVarsity Press, 2006.

Wright, Tom. *The Day the Revolution Began: Rethinking the Meaning of Jesus' Crucifixion*. London: SPCK, 2016.

———. *Paul: A Biography*. London: SPCK, 2018.

Žižek, Slavoj. "Thinking Backward: Predestination and Apocalypse." In Milbank, Žižek and Davis, *Paul's New Moment*, 185–190.

Žižek, Slavoj, and Boris Gunjevic. *God in Pain: Inversions of Apocalypse*. New York: Seven Stories, 2012.

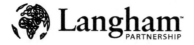

Langham Literature and its imprints are a ministry of Langham Partnership.

Langham Partnership is a global fellowship working in pursuit of the vision God entrusted to its founder John Stott –

> *to facilitate the growth of the church in maturity and Christ-likeness through raising the standards of biblical preaching and teaching.*

Our vision is to see churches in the majority world equipped for mission and growing to maturity in Christ through the ministry of pastors and leaders who believe, teach and live by the Word of God.

Our mission is to strengthen the ministry of the Word of God through:
* nurturing national movements for biblical preaching
* fostering the creation and distribution of evangelical literature
* enhancing evangelical theological education

especially in countries where churches are under-resourced.

Our ministry

Langham Preaching partners with national leaders to nurture indigenous biblical preaching movements for pastors and lay preachers all around the world. With the support of a team of trainers from many countries, a multi-level programme of seminars provides practical training, and is followed by a programme for training local facilitators. Local preachers' groups and national and regional networks ensure continuity and ongoing development, seeking to build vigorous movements committed to Bible exposition.

Langham Literature provides majority world preachers, scholars and seminary libraries with evangelical books and electronic resources through publishing and distribution, grants and discounts. The programme also fosters the creation of indigenous evangelical books in many languages, through writer's grants, strengthening local evangelical publishing houses, and investment in major regional literature projects, such as one volume Bible commentaries like *The Africa Bible Commentary* and *The South Asia Bible Commentary.*

Langham Scholars provides financial support for evangelical doctoral students from the majority world so that, when they return home, they may train pastors and other Christian leaders with sound, biblical and theological teaching. This programme equips those who equip others. Langham Scholars also works in partnership with majority world seminaries in strengthening evangelical theological education. A growing number of Langham Scholars study in high quality doctoral programmes in the majority world itself. As well as teaching the next generation of pastors, graduated Langham Scholars exercise significant influence through their writing and leadership.

To learn more about Langham Partnership and the work we do visit **langham.org**

CPSIA information can be obtained
at www.ICGtesting.com
Printed in the USA
LVHW081958130121
676047LV00008B/479

9 781783 687770